W9-CAR-064

MUSIC ESSENTIALS FOR CLASSROOM TEACHERS

Robert Pace
TEACHERS COLLEGE
COLUMBIA UNIVERSITY

WADSWORTH PUBLISHING COMPANY, INC.
BELMONT, CALIFORNIA

WADSWORTH MUSIC SERIES

BASIC PIANO FOR ADULTS by Helene Robinson

ENGLISH FOLK SONGS: SOME CONCLUSIONS, 3rd edition, by Cecil J. Sharp (edited by Maud Karpeles)

FIVE CENTURIES OF KEYBOARD MUSIC by John Gillespie

FOUNDATIONS IN MUSIC THEORY by Leon Dallin

MUSIC ESSENTIALS FOR CLASSROOM TEACHERS by Robert Pace

MUSIC IN THE EDUCATION OF CHILDREN, 2nd edition, by Bessie R. Swanson

SINGING WITH CHILDREN by Robert Nye, Vernice Nye, Neva Aubin, and George Kyme

TALKING ABOUT CONCERTOS by Antony Hopkins

TALKING ABOUT SYMPHONIES by Antony Hopkins

TEACHING MUSIC IN THE SECONDARY SCHOOLS by Charles R. Hoffer

L.C. Cat. Card No.: 61-9017
Printed in the United States of America

FIRST PRINTING: MAY 1961
SECOND PRINTING: MARCH 1962
THIRD PRINTING: JULY 1964

FOREWORD

To teach music is to promote its understanding and enjoyment, to share our knowledge and enthusiasm with others. Emerson has truly said that "man may teach by doing, and not otherwise." This book provides the means for "doing." It explains the grammar of music in simple terms, promotes musical literacy, and provides essential knowledge for the teaching of music to children.

Teachers and students alike learn by doing, that is, *from experience*. This book provides such experience in singing, playing, and understanding music. It shows the teacher how to read, accompany, and explain songs for classroom use, as well as to create them.

The classroom teacher needs such knowledge for both professional competence and personal satisfaction. Actually, the language of music is simple when learned through experience geared to both personal and professional needs. Here is a book that does relate learning to needs, and theory to practice. It gives the classroom teacher, and others, a functional musical background, and makes learning a rewarding experience, not a meaningless task.

HOWARD A. MURPHY
EDITOR

PREFACE

The purpose of this book is to give classroom teachers and other interested adults an understanding of music fundamentals. The basic structure of music (chords, melodies, rhythms, and forms) may be analyzed and understood whether found in the classroom, the concert hall, or the home. Music theory in its more technical aspects may seem unnecessary to the person who has limited time for acquiring musical background and performance skill. It is for this reason that an "applied activity" approach is used here. Each musical idea is related to the learner's background and refers immediately to some authentic situation so that skill and understanding can come from actual application. Thus music becomes a usable, practical part of the student's background. Musical nomenclature is introduced only as it is needed. As a result, some things may be passed over at first, but clarified later. Occasionally some musical explanations are avoided, since they might confuse the student at that point.

Those individuals who have confidence in their ability and have enjoyed success in their music studies will be most likely to use music in later life—either in their profession or for their own personal satisfaction. This is not to presume that everyone will want to sing or that everyone will want to play an instrument. It is assumed, however, that everyone can derive greater enjoyment from music if he has some knowledge of its structure.

Why should the nonprofessional music lover or classroom teacher study music fundamentals? Isn't it possible to teach music or to enjoy it—at least on a superficial level—without any specific knowledge of its rules and regulations? Perhaps, but to a limited degree. The educational aim in any field should be to increase the individual's capacity for accomplishment and enjoyment as the natural result of understanding. Thus, for the classroom teacher, the principal, or the music specialist, knowledge of the fundamentals of music not only fulfills a professional requirement but also provides a means for greater personal enjoyment.

CONTENTS

3

4

5

6

MUSIC ESSENTIALS FOR CLASSROOM TEACHERS

1

Melody Patterns

In this book you will learn about the basic elements of music: *melody*, *rhythm*, *harmony*, and *form*. Since everyone has sung, hummed, and whistled various tunes it is logical to begin our discussion with *melodies*. Reading musical notation involves recognizing melodic patterns and seeing the contour of a melodic line. To recognize these patterns, remember that melodies either:

a. move down
b. move up
c. repeat the same tone

This excerpt from "Joy to the World" illustrates the downward movement of a melody.

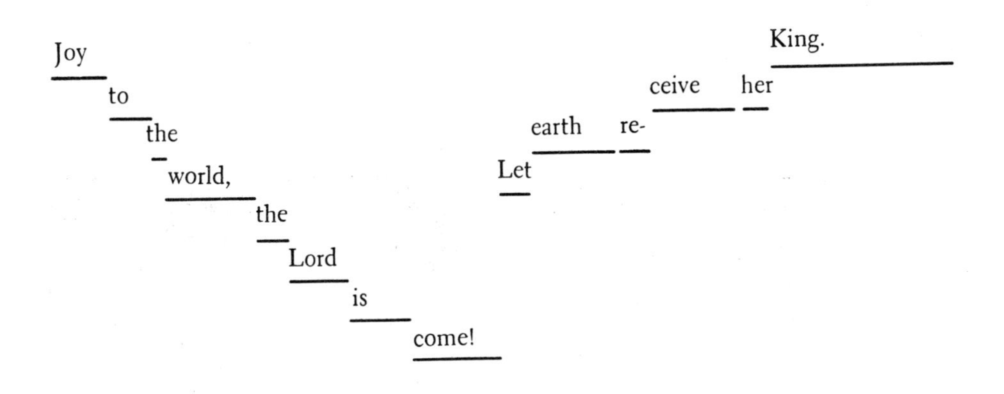

In "Oh Susanna" we see a melody with frequent changes of direction—both up and down. Sing this now as your hand shows the "shape" of the melodic line in the air.

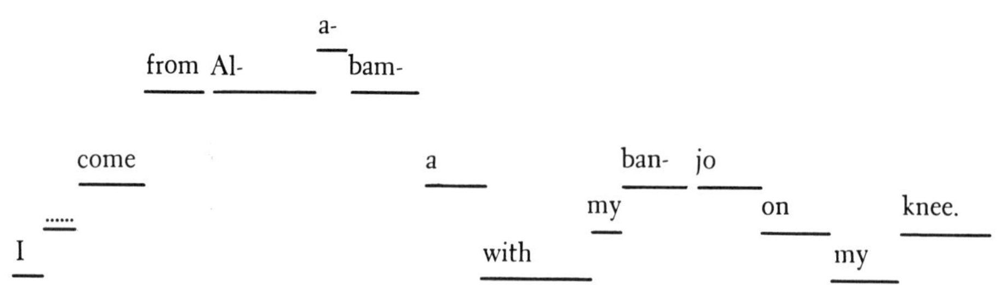

Our third melody, "Jingle Bells," shows repeated tones as well as upward and downward melodic movement. As you sing and shape this one, notice that certain pitches seem closer than others. Sometimes the melody "skips" and sometimes it just "goes next door."

gle

Jin- gle bells! Jin- gle bells! Jin- way!

the

all

To visualize more clearly the skips and repeated tones in the movement of these melodies, play each tune on the melody bells or piano as you sing. You may use your index finger to pick them out on the piano.

JOY TO THE WORLD

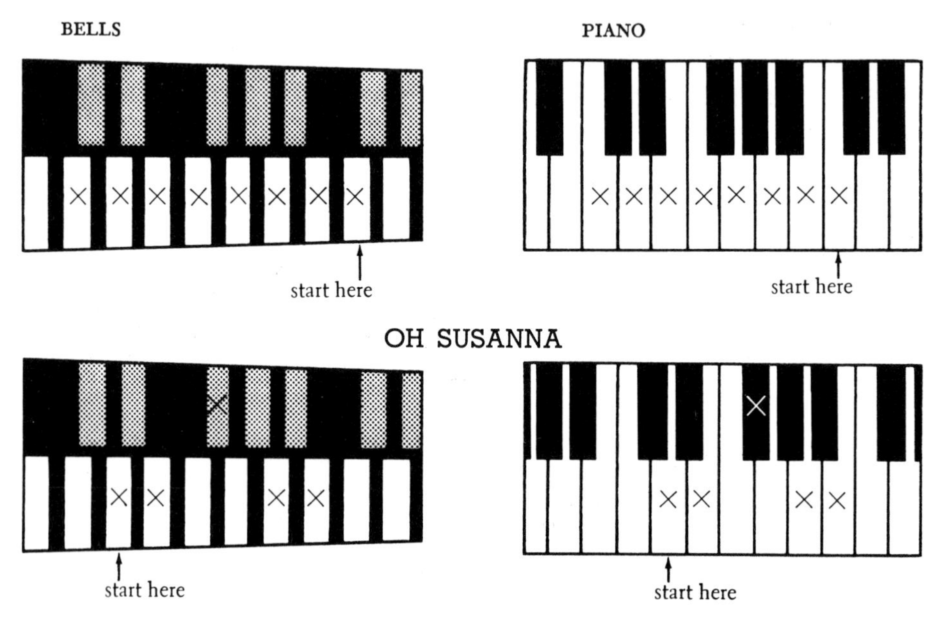

JINGLE BELLS

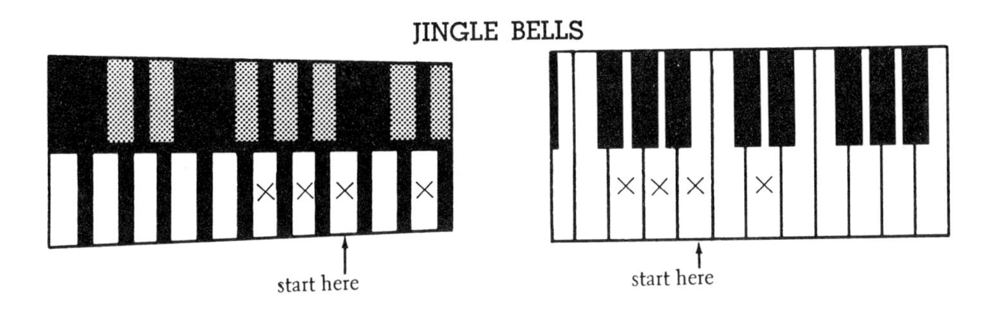

Now you are ready to name the lines and spaces of the *Grand Staff* and to identify the pitches of the songs you have just sung.

The Grand Staff

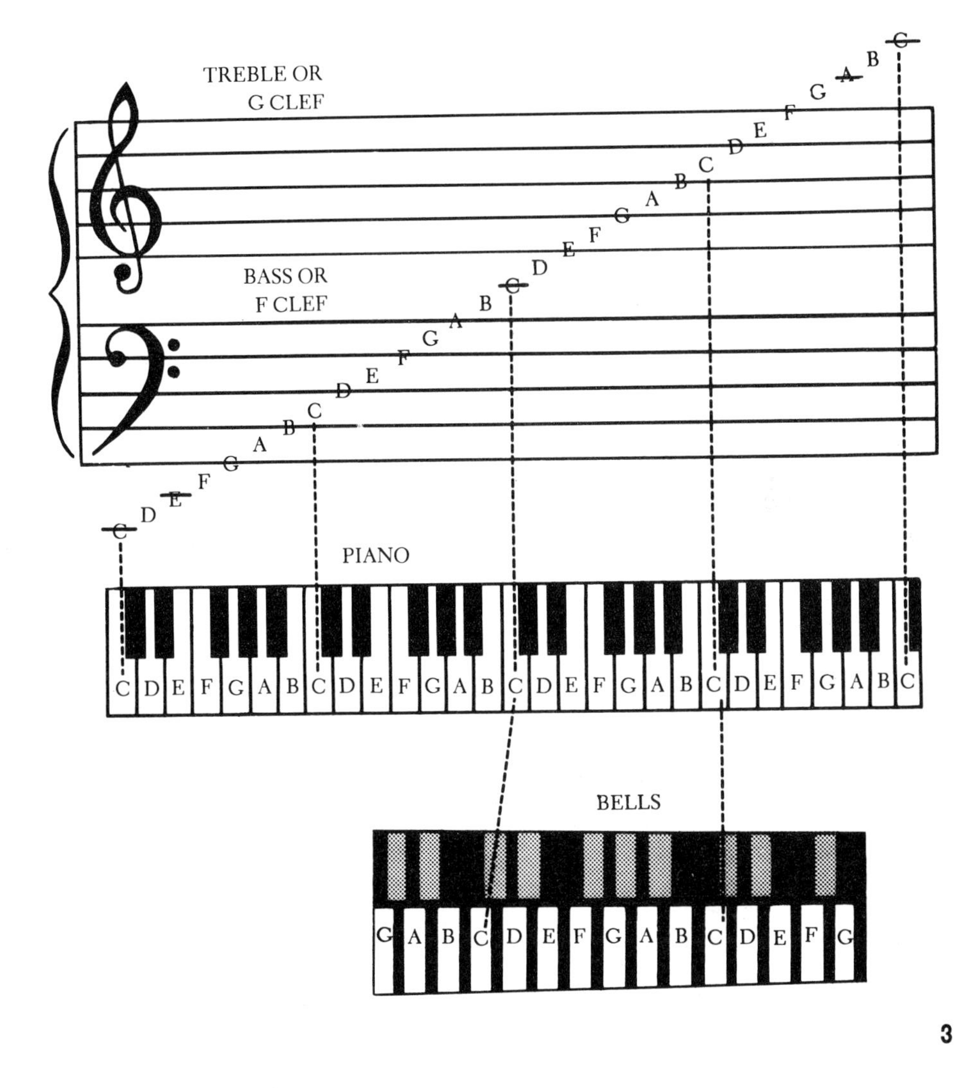

Here are the tones of "Joy to the World" as you have sung them:

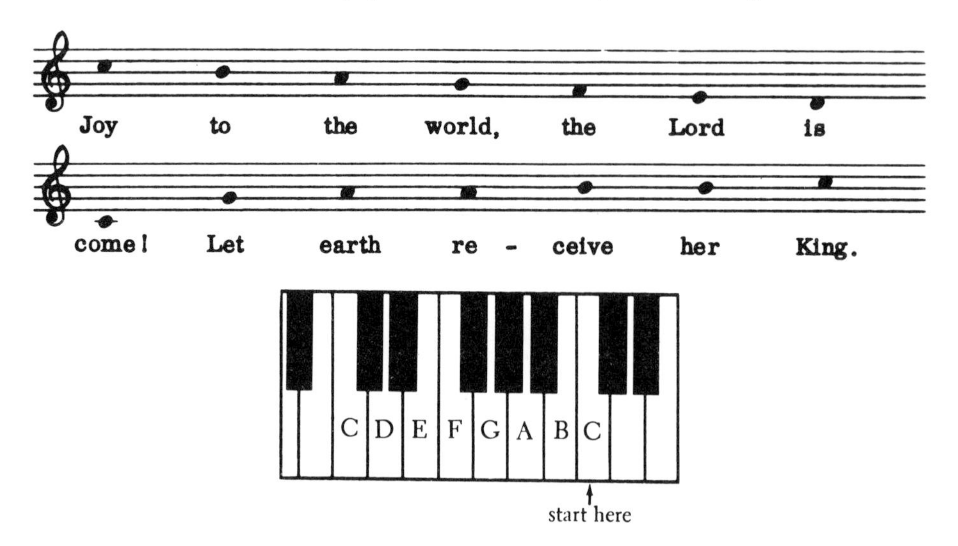

If you were to start on F, this song would be too low for most voices, especially children's:

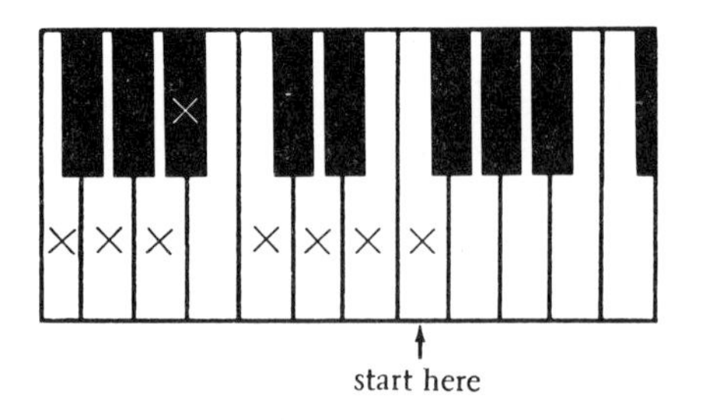

You have sung "Oh Susanna" beginning on D. But if you were to start on A, you would probably find it too high. In any song, there are certain tones that are more comfortable to sing than others.

With the syllable "loo," sing the following five tones as you play them on the melody bells or piano. Do this several times beginning on C until you have the sound "in your ear."

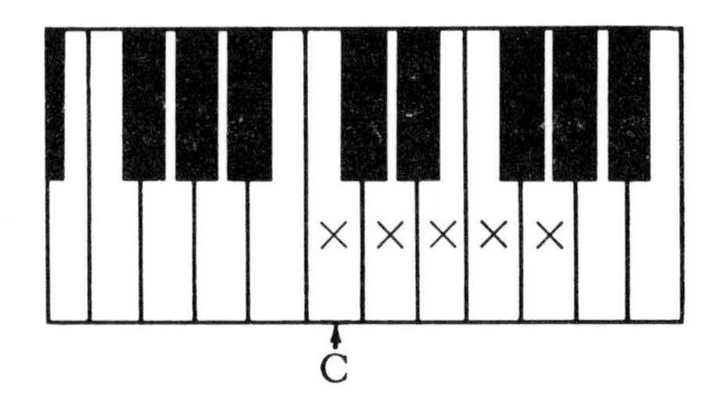

Then play D and sing the five tones upward *without* the melody bells or piano. Finally play the tones while you sing. Watch for the note that must be changed, and mark with an X the notes you have played.

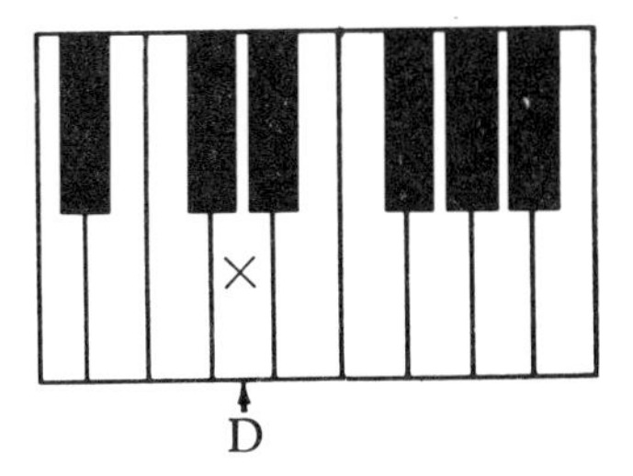

The five-tone melody you have just sung consists of a series of *whole steps* and *half steps.* Your ear helps you sing the same succession of whole steps and half steps, whether you started on C, D, or E.

The distance between any two tones is called an *interval.* A *half step* (the smallest interval) is the distance from any tone to the very next one above or below:

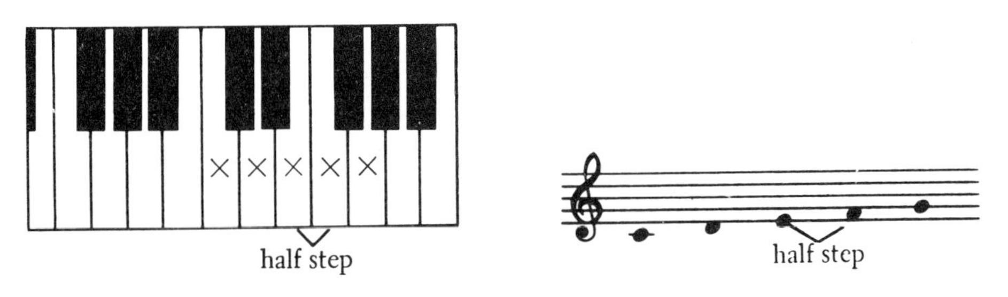

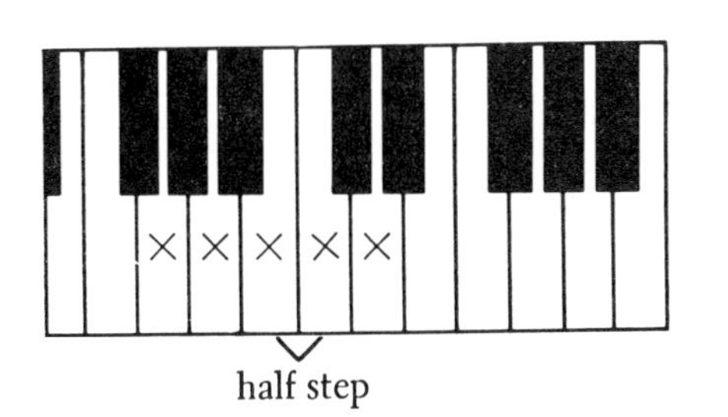

A *whole step* is any combination of two consecutive half steps:

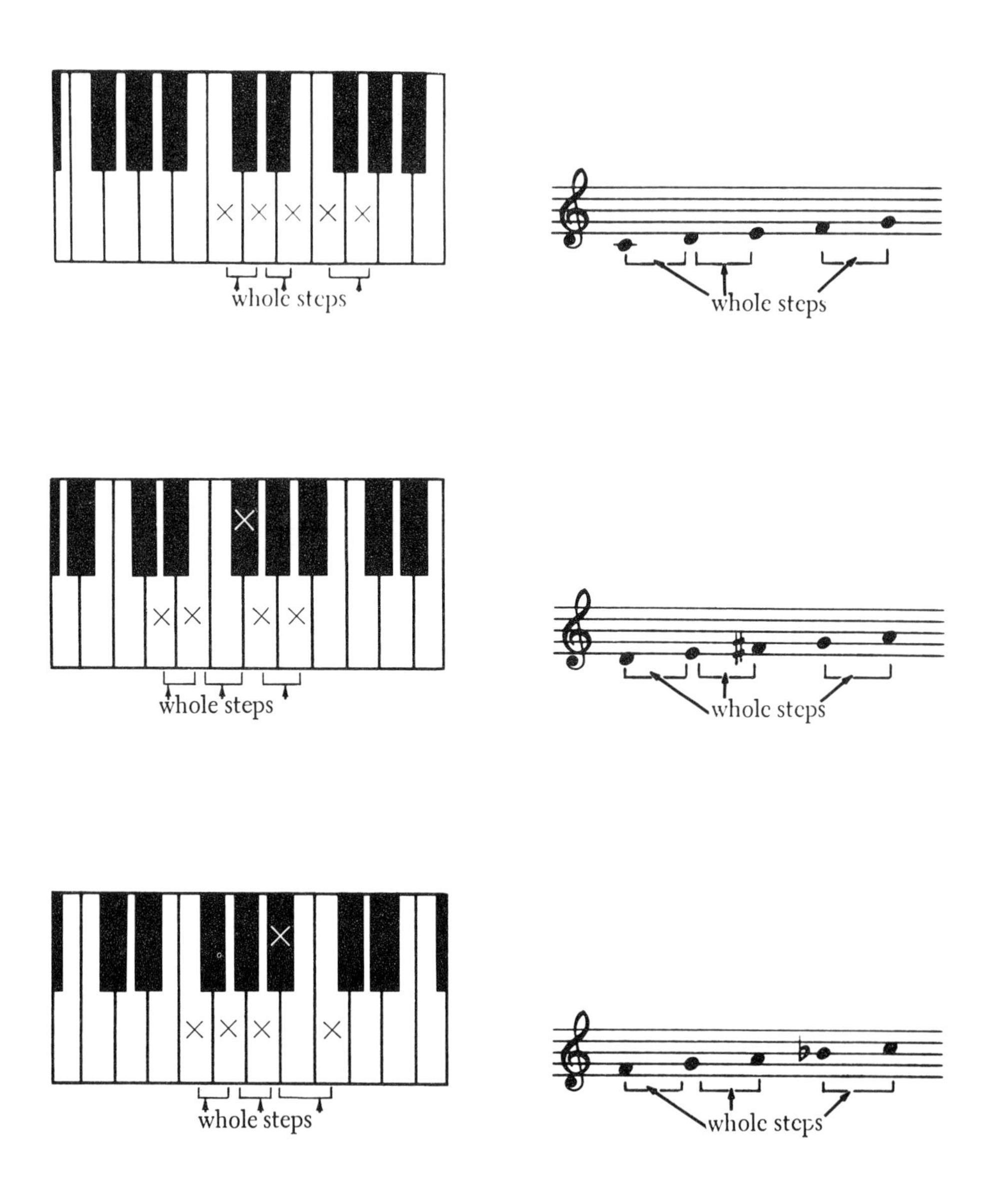

Notice that when we began on D or F we could no longer use only white keys to maintain the correct sequence of half and whole steps. It was necessary to add *sharps* and *flats* to the note to maintain the correct relation of half and whole steps. A sharp (♯) raises the pitch one half step:

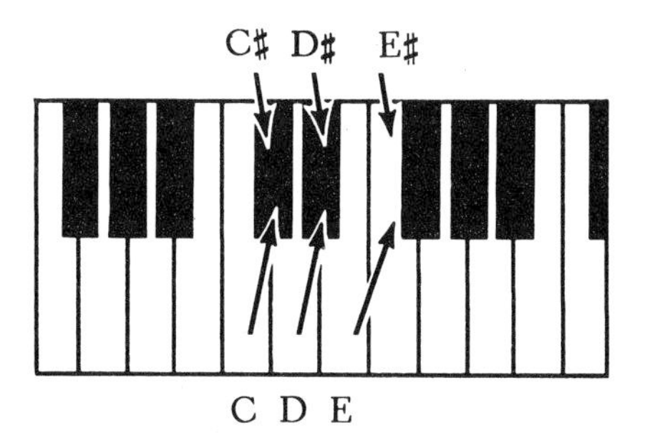

A flat (♭) lowers it one half step:

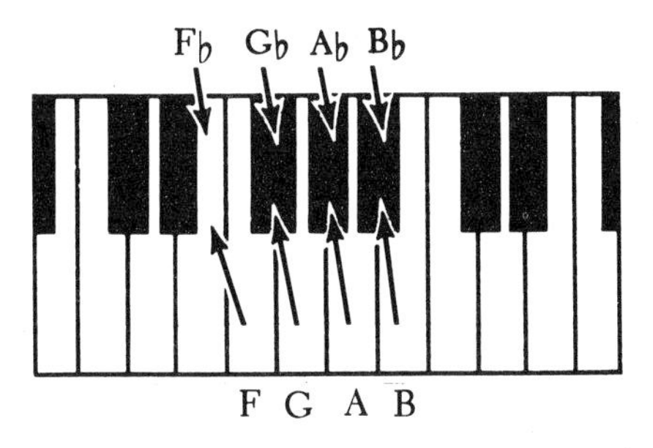

Major Scale

The arrangement of whole and half steps such as the opening eight tones of "Joy to the World" is a major scale.

Descending scale (C):

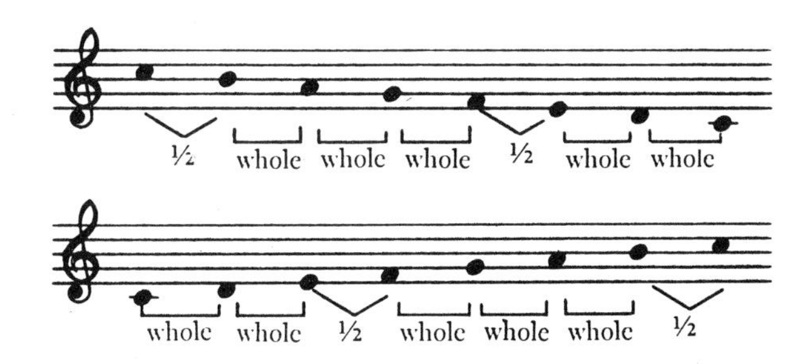

Ascending scale (C):

All major scales have the same sequence of whole and half steps.

Key Signatures

At the beginning of each score of music there is a *key signature*, which tells those tones to be sharped or flatted in the scale of that song. To identify any major key signature with sharps, *count up one letter name from the last sharp*. The name of any major key signature with flats takes its name from the *next to last flat*. Remember that the key with one flat is F major. Here are the *major* key signatures and scales for the seven sharp keys:

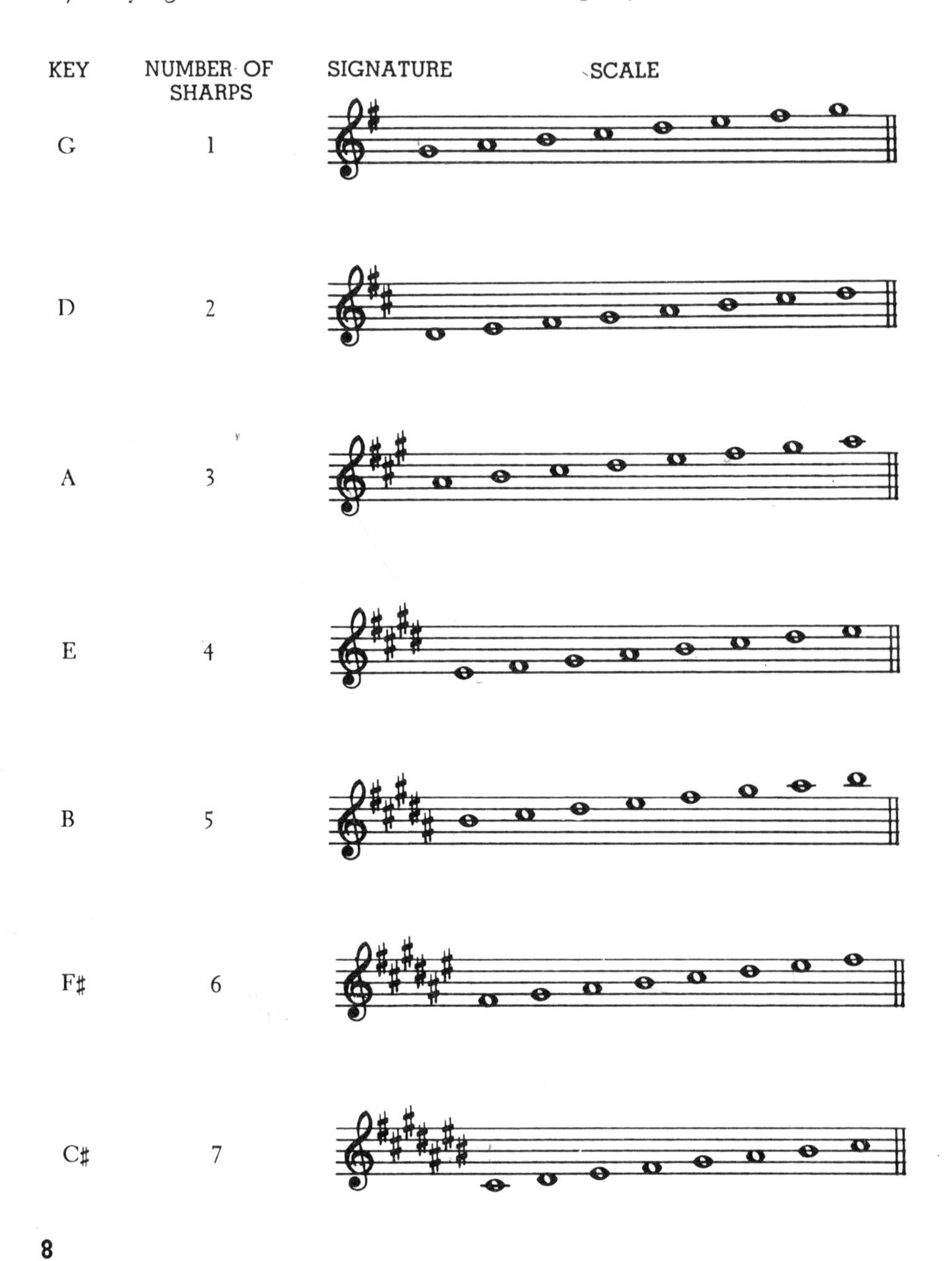

Here are the major key signatures and scales for the seven flat keys:

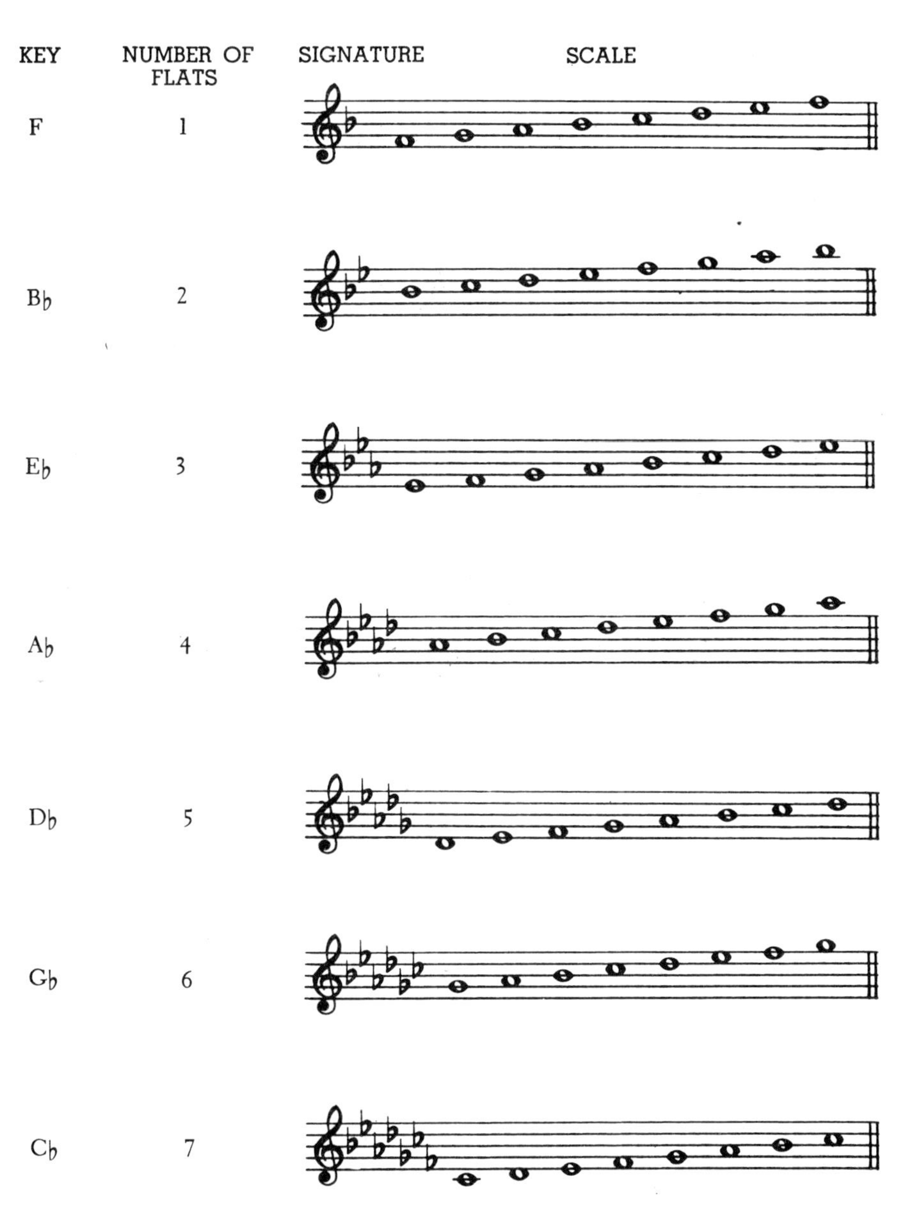

Time Signatures

Immediately following the key signature at the beginning of any song there is a *time signature:*

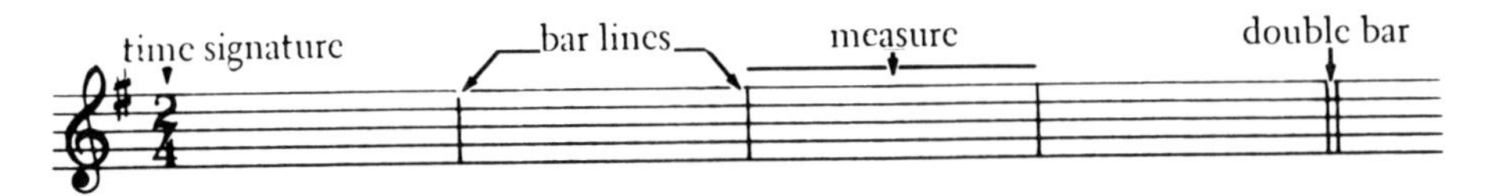

The top number of the time signature shows the *number of beats* or pulsations in each measure, while the bottom number tells *what kind of note* (or its equivalent) *receives one beat,* or *count.* A measure is a unit for measuring time in music, its limits being defined by bar lines.

Rhythm

So far we have discussed only the pitch but not the duration of a note. Here again is a small part of "Joy to the World." Sing and clap it as you notice the rhythm.

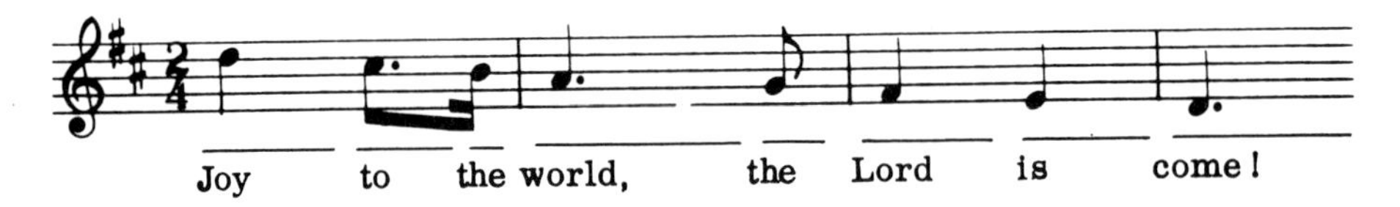

The head of the note locates the pitch, while the color of the note (black or white), stems, flags, and dots show the duration of the note. (A dot increases any note or rest by one-half its original value.) Here is a chart of some of the most frequently used note values with their equivalent rests or periods of silence.

SYMBOLS OF DURATION

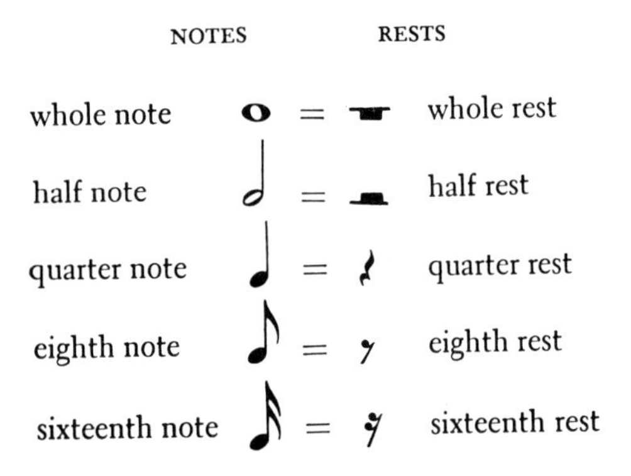

Remember that every measure in a song must have the number of beats designated by the top number. This number of beats may consist of any combination of note values, so long as their total is the same as the top number. In musical notation you will find eighth and sixteenth notes written either of the ways shown here.

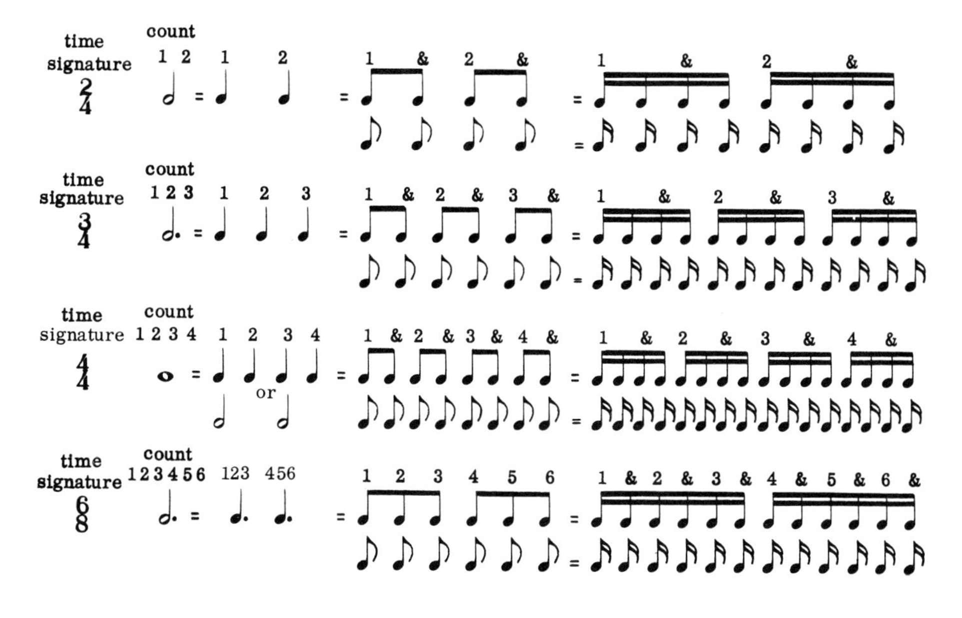

Melodic Patterns

To become proficient at reading music, one should be able to recognize melodic patterns as they are related to the *degrees* of a scale. The degrees of any major scale are numbered from the keynote (commonly referred to as "do") upward to the next keynote. For example:

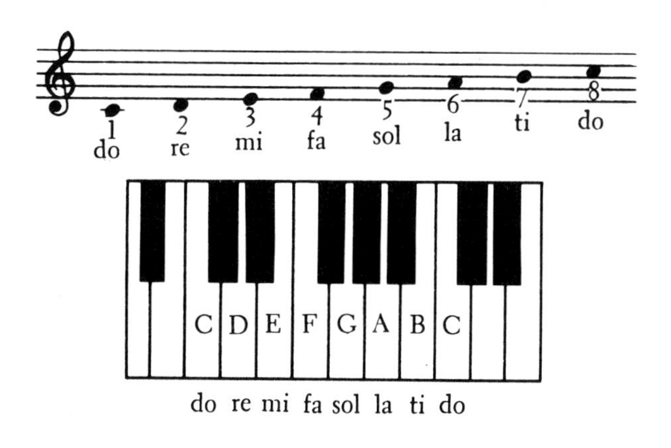

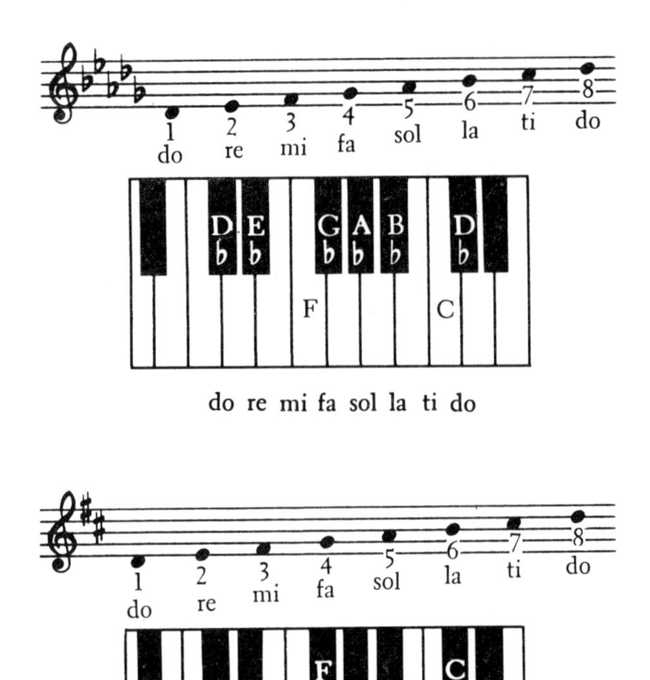

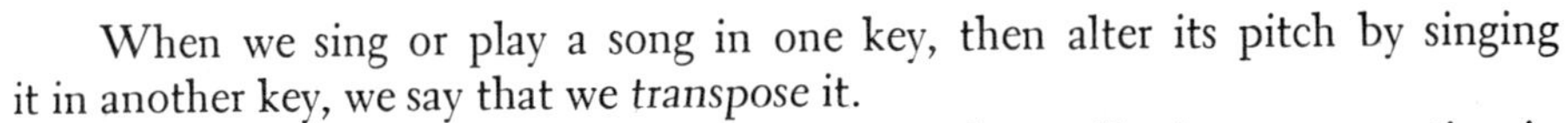

When we sing or play a song in one key, then alter its pitch by singing it in another key, we say that we *transpose* it.

Here are fragments of well-known songs that will give you practice in recognizing some of the most common melodic patterns. Transpose them, first starting one tone higher, then one tone lower.

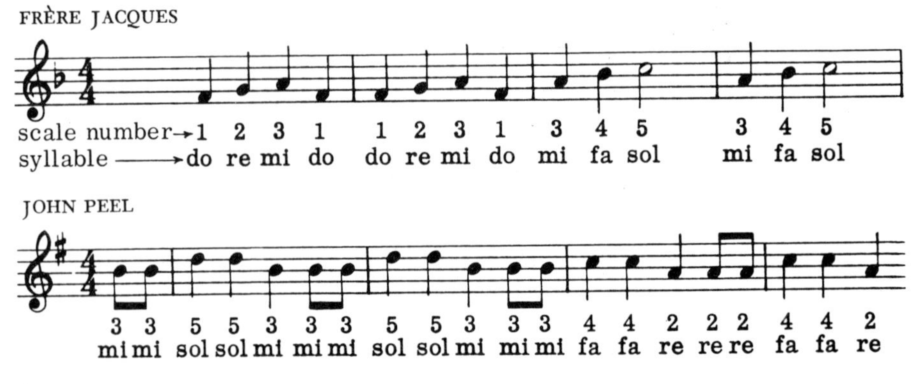

THE FIRST NOEL
3 2 1 2 3 4 5 6 7 8 7 6 5
mi re do re mi fa sol la ti do ti la sol
LI'L LIZA JANE
3 3 2 1 3 5 5 6 5 3 5
mi mi re do mi sol sol la sol mi sol
BILLY BOY
3 4 5 5 5 8 3 4 5 5 6 5
mi fa sol sol sol do mi fa sol sol la sol
CHORUS—BATTLE HYMN OF THE REPUBLIC
5 4 3 5 8 2 3 8 6 7 8 7 8 6 5 3
sol fa mi sol do re mi do la ti do ti do la sol mi
SILENT NIGHT
5 6 5 3 5 6 5 3 2 2 7 1 1 5
sol la sol mi sol la sol mi re re ti do do sol
BLOW THE MAN DOWN
5 5 6 5 3 1 3 5 6 5 3
sol sol la sol mi do mi sol la sol mi
THEME—HAYDN "SURPRISE" SYMPHONY
1 1 3 3 5 5 3 4 4 2 2 7 7 5
do do mi mi sol sol mi fa fa re re ti ti sol
OLD MACDONALD
1 1 1 5 6 6 5 3 3 2 2 1
do do do sol la la sol mi mi re re do

Intervals

In learning to read musical symbols, ask yourself the following questions:

a. Does the melody go by steps (line-space-line-space, etc.)?

Or does it skip (line-line-line)?

Or space-space-space, etc.?

b. What is the interval? Does it skip up a 3rd?

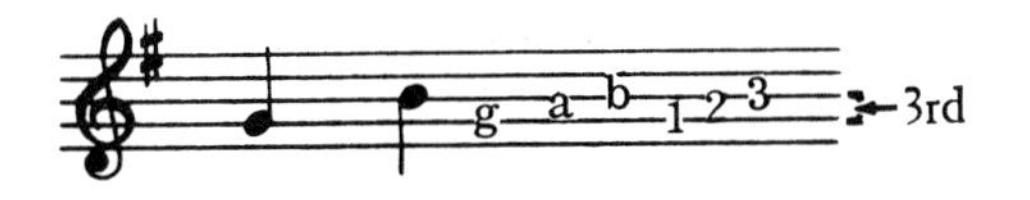

Up a 4th?

Down a 5th?

etc.

In determining the number name (size) of the interval, always be sure to count the bottom note as "one."

In any major key, using "do" as "one," 2nds, 3rds, 6ths, and 7ths are called *major* intervals. 1sts (unisons), 4ths, 5ths, and 8ths (octaves) are called *perfect* intervals.

Major intervals lowered one half step become *minor*, and perfect intervals lowered one half step become *diminished*.

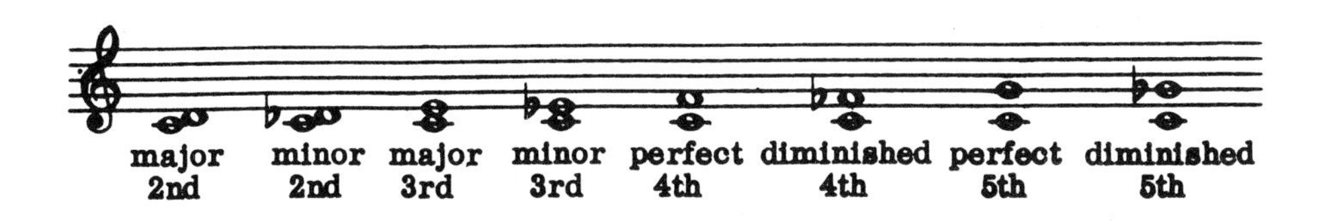

Major and perfect intervals raised one half step become *augmented*.

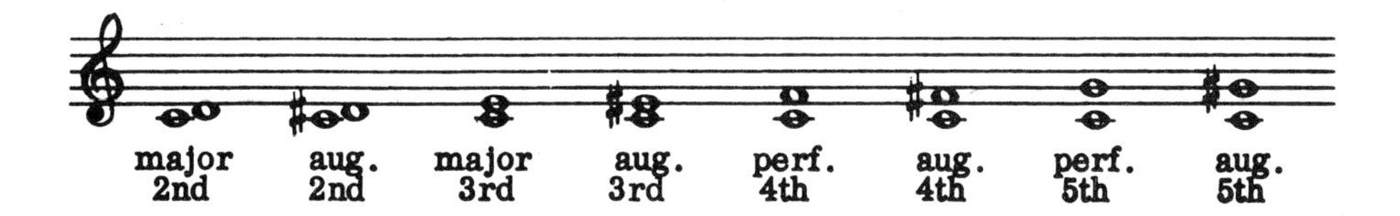

Always think of the interval in terms of the key signature of the lower note to determine whether it is major, minor, perfect, augmented, or diminished. Therefore,

E to G♯ is a major 3rd since there is a G♯ in the key signature and scale of E major, while E to G would be a minor 3rd.

The I Chord

In the first four measures of "Little Tom Tinker" the ascending melody line uses the first, third, and fifth degrees of the scale.

These three tones played simultaneously are called a *chord* or *triad* (meaning three-tone chord) when arranged line-line-line or space-space-space. Always number the tones of the chord from the bottom up, root, third, and fifth.

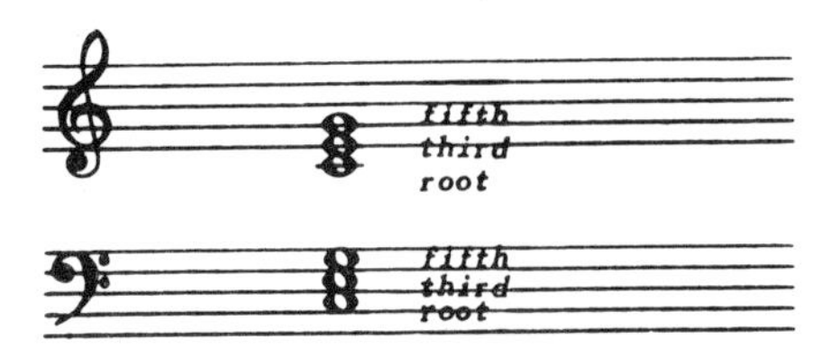

The triad built on the first degree of the scale of any key is called the I (one) chord or the *tonic* chord.

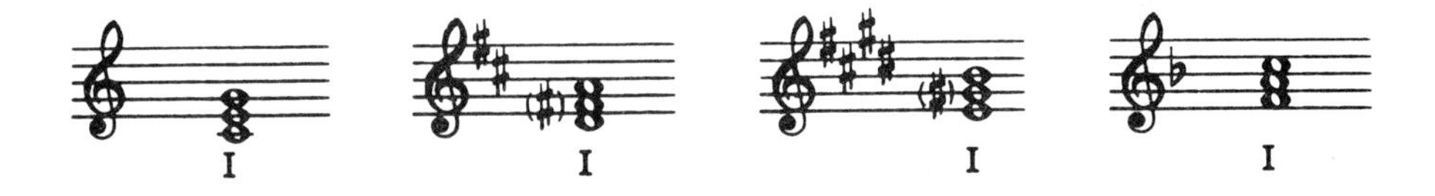

On the Autoharp or piano, find the C major chord (I chord) and play it as an accompaniment for "Little Tom Tinker."

LITTLE TOM TINKER

Old Round

When two successive notes of the same pitch are connected by a curved line, as they are in the accompaniment of "Little Tom Tinker," the second note is not repeated. The curved line is a *tie*. The *slur*, as found in the fifth and sixth measure, is an indication to phrase the notes smoothly (*legato*).

Now try "Frère Jacques" with an F chord. Notice that the I chord is played on the first beat of the measure when a tone from that chord (a chord tone) appears in the melody.

FRÈRE JACQUES

French Folk Song

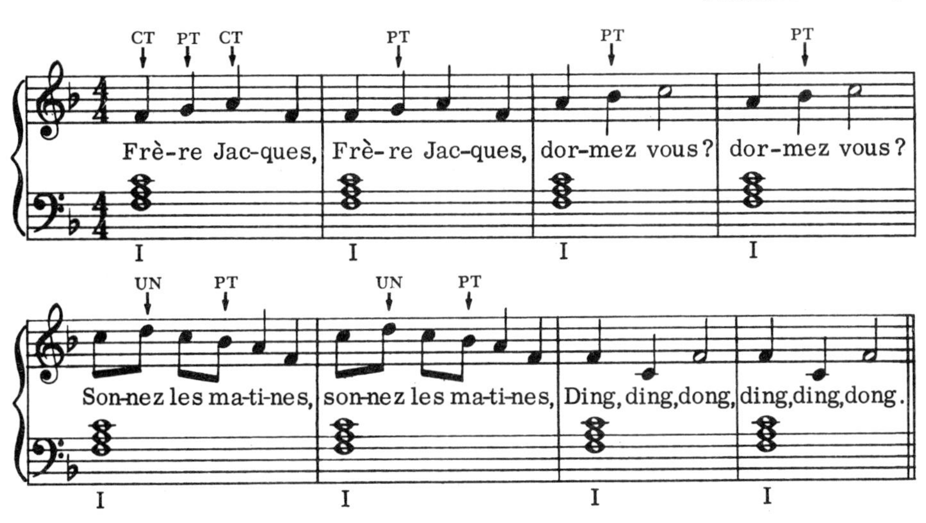

Between these *chord tones* (CT) are *passing tones* (PT), which connect chord tones by stepwise progression. In the fifth and seventh measures the D is an *upper neighbor* (UN) since it is immediately above the chord tone. A note below a chord tone would be a *lower neighbor* (LN).

Now you have learned something about melody, rhythm, and harmony. The following supplementary material is designed to help you gain greater skill and better understanding of these basic elements of music.

FOR FURTHER STUDY

1. Sing and "shape" the following familiar melodies using the syllable "loo." Check yourself with melody bells or piano to see whether you are visualizing properly the stepwise progressions and the skips.

   "America"
   "Auld Lang Syne"
   "Old MacDonald Had a Farm"

2. On the piano or bells, play these melodies as written.

MARY HAD A LITTLE LAMB

Nursery Tune

OATS, PEAS, BEANS

Singing Game

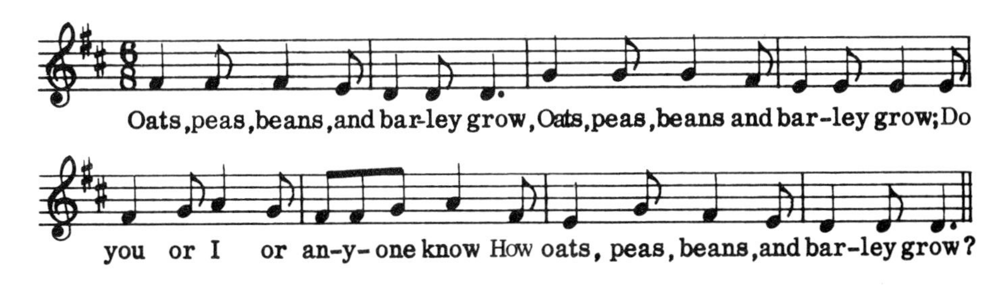

3. Fill in the lines of the grand staff.

Fill in the spaces of the grand staff.

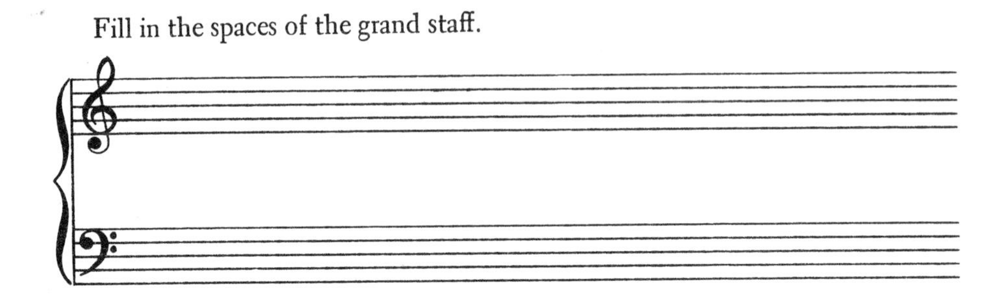

4. Fill in the missing notes of these familiar songs.

I SAW THREE SHIPS

English Folk Song

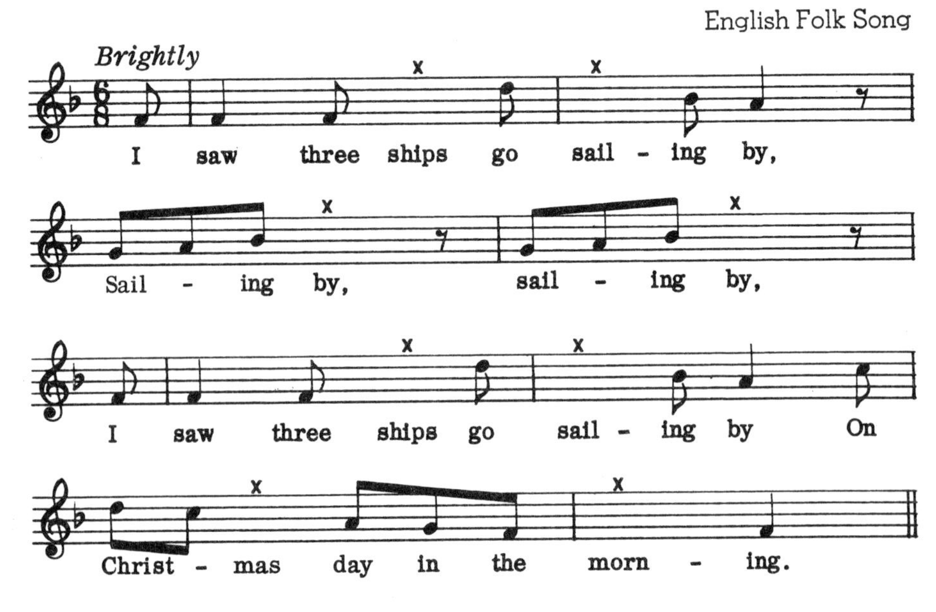

SUSIE, LITTLE SUSIE

German Folk Song

SHE'LL BE COMIN' 'ROUND THE MOUNTAIN

American Folk Song

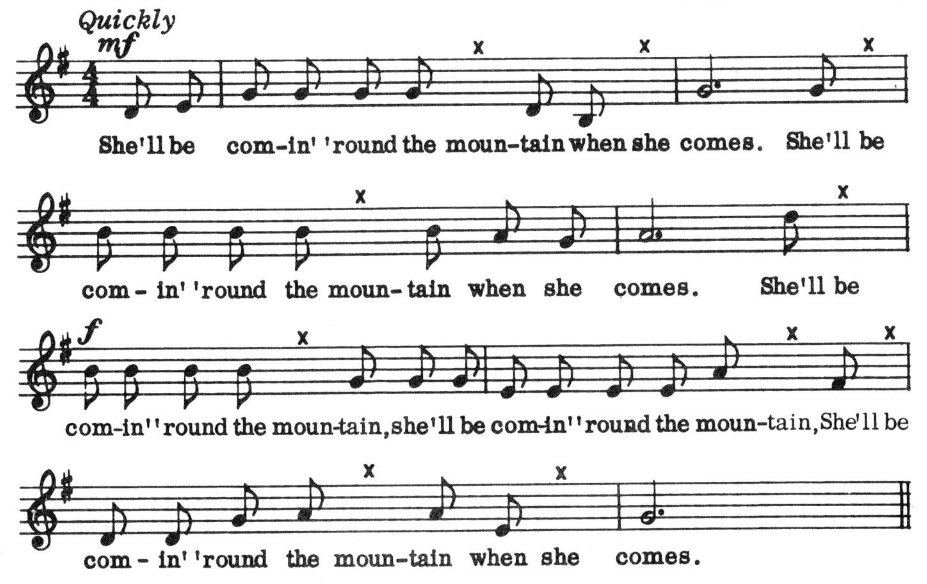

5. Write all major flat and sharp key signatures.

Supply the correct notes for these scales, then play on the melody bells or piano.

Key of D♭

Key of E

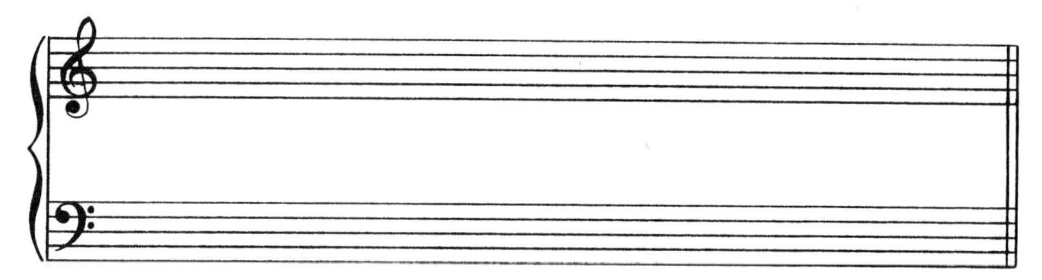

Key of A

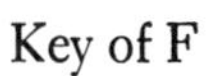

Key of F

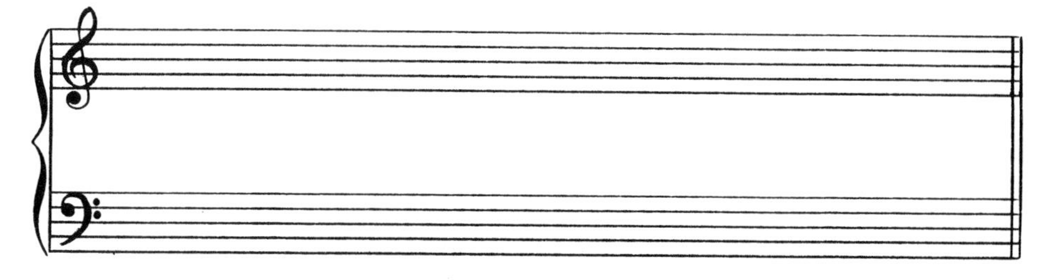

6. Fill in the correct time signatures for these melodies.

7. Transpose these melodies as indicated; then sing each with "loo."

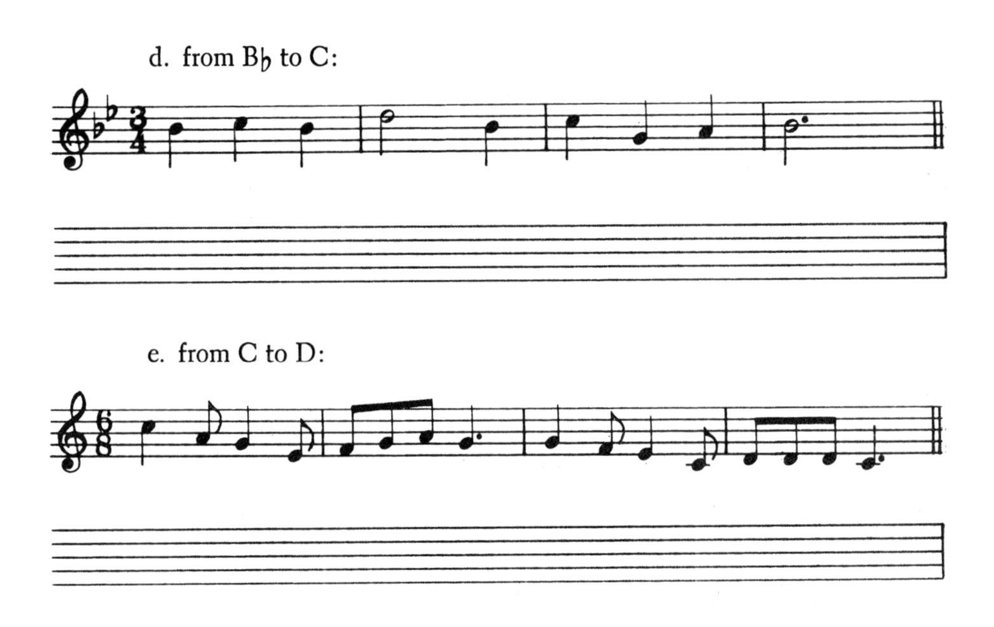

8. Mark these intervals as either half steps or whole steps.

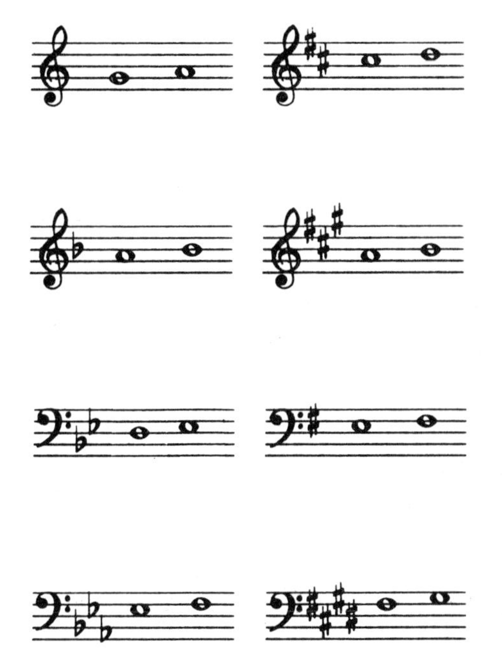

9. Clap or play the following rhythms.

10. Name these intervals as major 2nds, minor 3rds, perfect 4ths, etc.

11. Sight-read by singing or playing the following songs.

12. Play the C, F, G, and B♭ major chords on the Autoharp or piano.

DIAGRAM OF THE AUTOHARP'S CHORD MECHANISM*

Press the buttons down with the left hand using the pointer finger on the tonic chord.

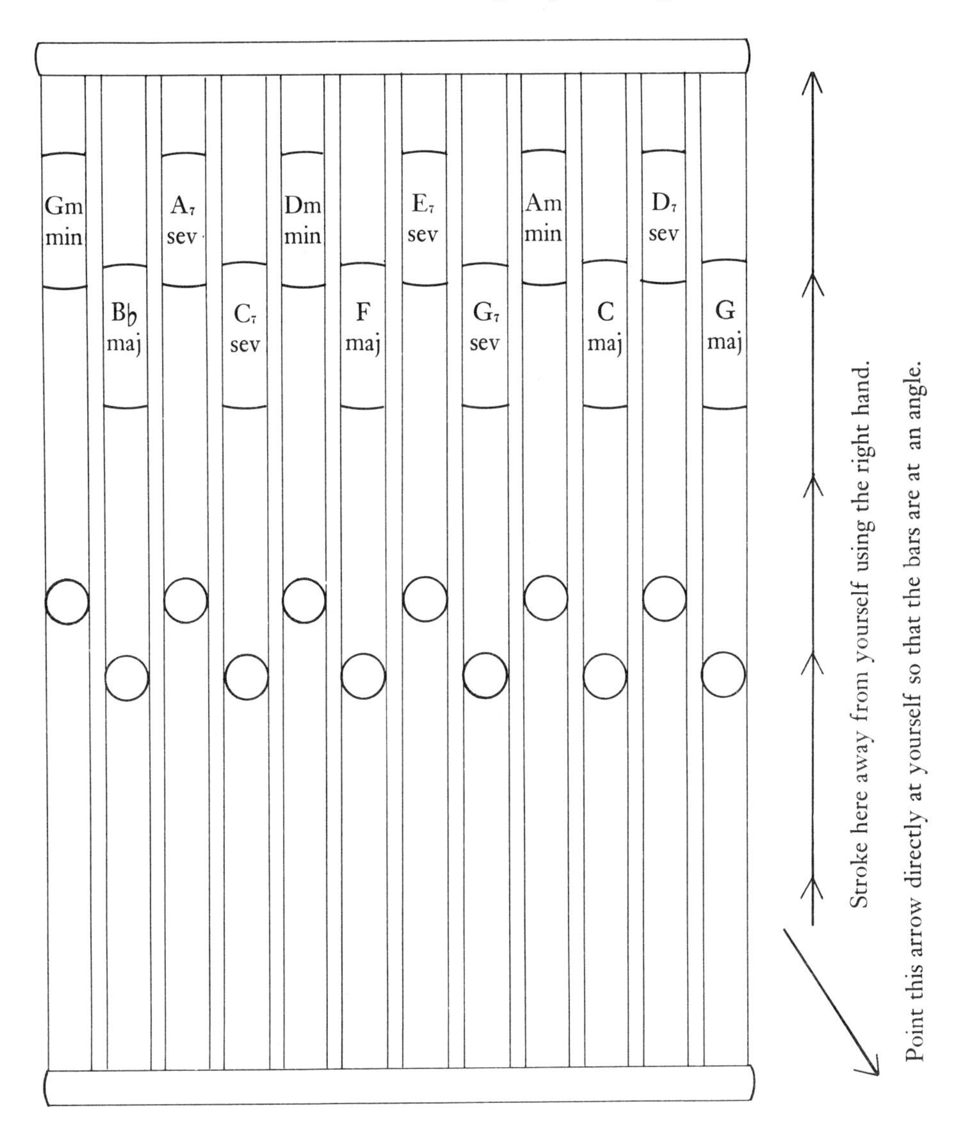

* Autoharp is the registered trade-mark of Oscar Schmidt-International, Inc.

13. Tell what each number means in the following time signatures:

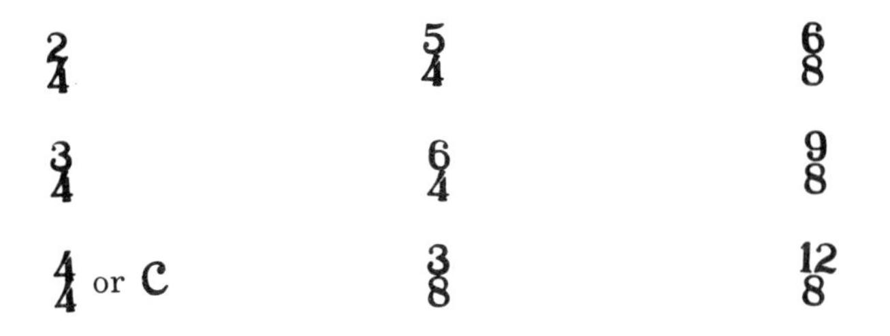

14. Label the passing tones (PT), upper neighbors (UN), and lower neighbors (LN) in this melody.

ROW, ROW, ROW YOUR BOAT

American Folk Song

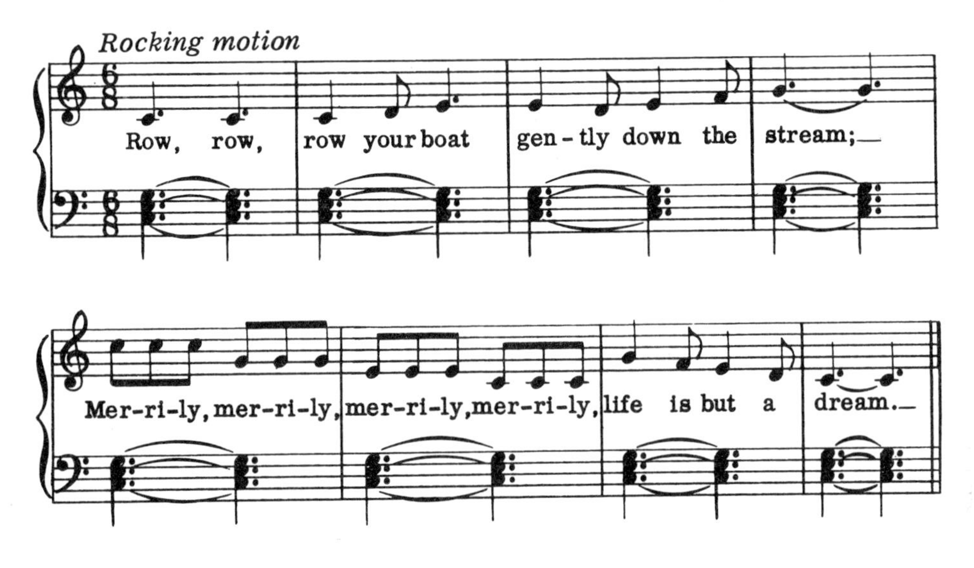

15. Identify the following melodies and insert the appropriate elements (stems, dots, flags) to make the correct rhythm.

2

The I and V_7 Chords

Although there are simple songs that can be harmonized with only the I chord, more than a single chord is needed to produce any feeling of harmonic motion and interest. Listen to "Mary Had a Little Lamb" harmonized with the I chord only.

In the third measure and the seventh measure your ear will tell you immediately that the I chord is not the best chord to use here.

A chord that would harmonize with the melody in these measures is the V_7 or *dominant seventh* chord. Just as the root of the I chord is found on the first degree of the scale, the root of the V_7 chord is found on the fifth degree of the scale. Notice that this chord has four tones in it in contrast to the three tones of the I chord.

Key of F:

I F — V7 C7 — or — I F — V7 C7

Key of C:

I C — V7 G7 — or — I C — V7 G7

Key of G:

I G — V7 D7 — or — I G — V7 D7

The Roman numerals refer to the degree of the scale on which the root of the chord is found. The chord may also be called by the letter name of the root (see example above). Arabic numerals refer to tones in a particular chord. Therefore, the designation V_7 or C_7 in the key of F means that the seventh tone above C will be present in that chord.

Inversion of the V_7 Chord

In simple classroom "chording," the V_7 is used most frequently in an inverted form with one note omitted.[1] It thereby progresses more smoothly to and from other triads. We shall use this inverted form of the chord and call it the V_7.

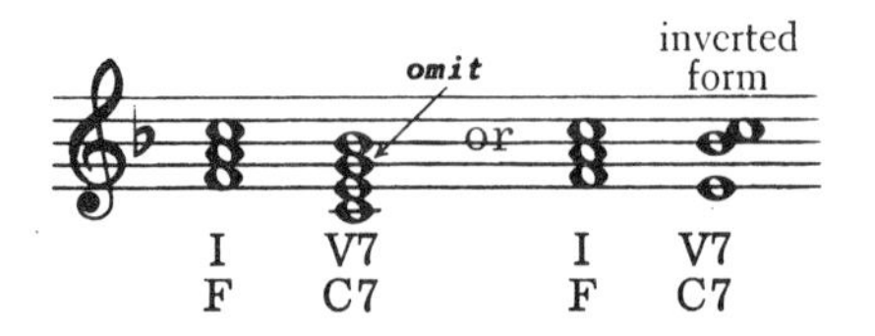

To go from the I chord to the V_7 chord on the piano remember that:

a. The bottom note *moves down one half step.*
b. The middle note *moves up one half step.*
c. The top note *remains the same.*

Practice finding the I and V_7 chords on the Autoharp and piano. Use this chording for piano:

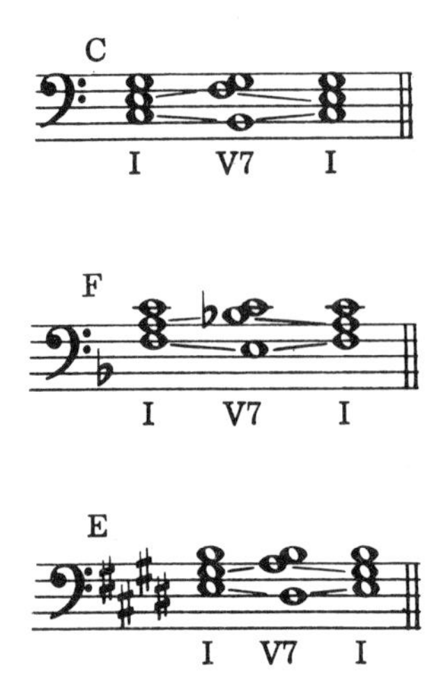

---

[1] Technically, it is referred to in this inversion as a V^6_5, the subscripts again identifying the position of the tones in relation to the bottom note of the chord:

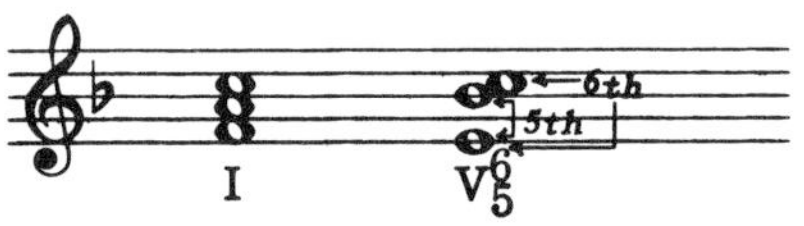

Harmonizing Melodies with the I and V_7 Chords

Sing these melodies and harmonize them with the I and V_7 chords on the Autoharp or piano. Notice the curved lines (⁀) above or below the notes. These lines are called "phrase markings" or slurs and are used to show melodic or rhythmic groupings.

SALLY GO ROUND

English Singing Game

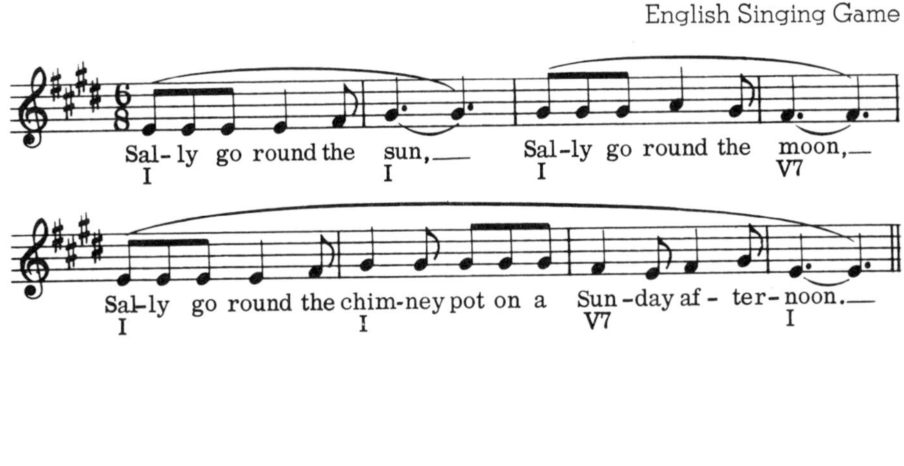

SUSIE, LITTLE SUSIE

Humperdinck

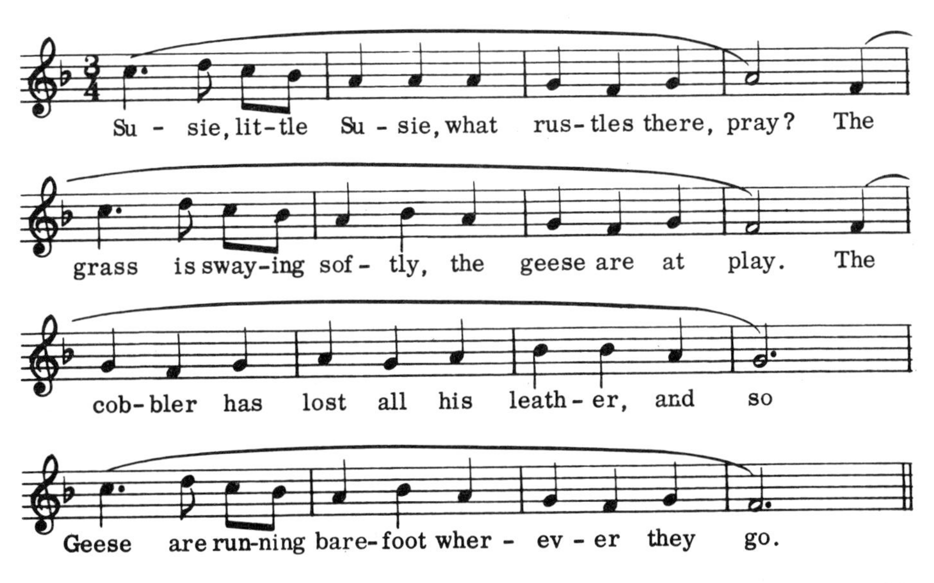

POLLY WOLLY DOODLE

American Song

Notice the use of chord tones, and also of non-chord tones such as passing tones and upper neighbors. Circle and label all non-chord tones.

As we have seen, melodies are constructed from chord tones, upper neighbors, lower neighbors, and passing tones. Now create you own melodies. Use *only* chord tones from the I and V_7 chords as in this example.

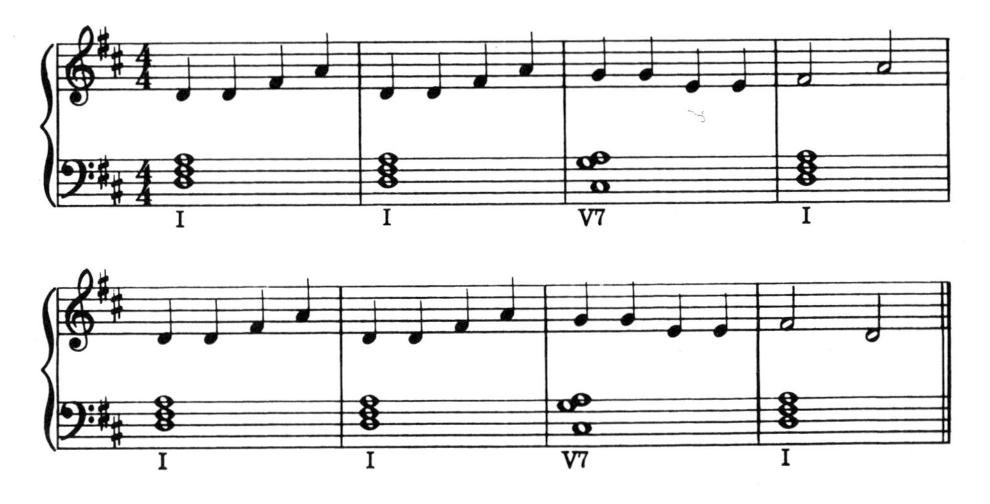

Try to use the same melodic idea in the fifth measure as you did in the first measure. This repetition will give the second part a feeling of continuity from the first.

After you have written the melody and harmony, either play your song on the piano or have two people play it—one on the Autoharp for harmony and the other on bells for melody.

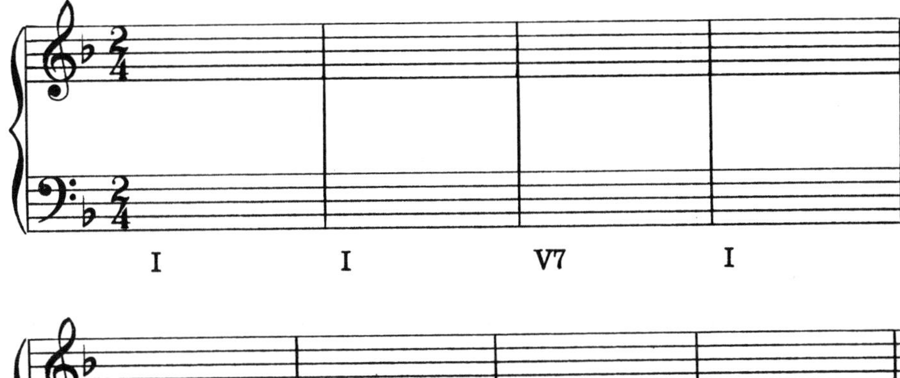

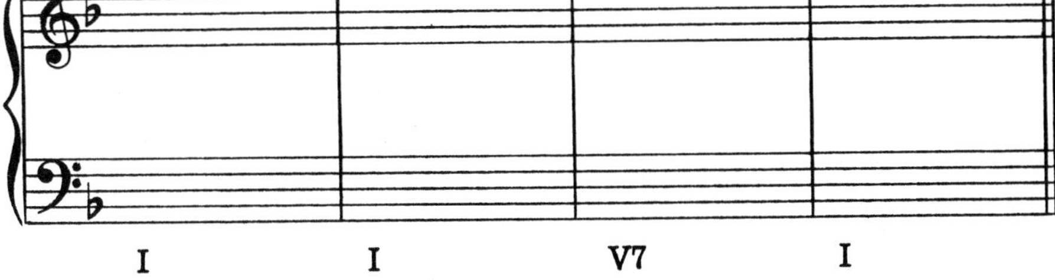

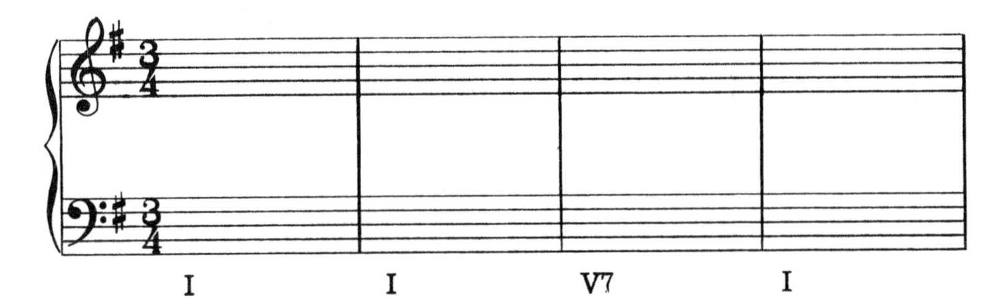
I
I
V7
I

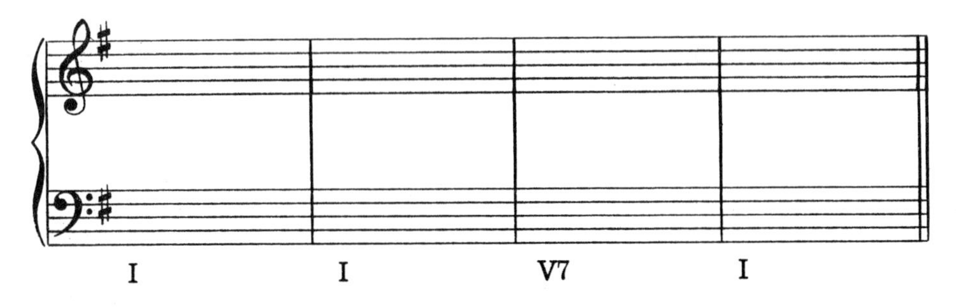
I
I
V7
I

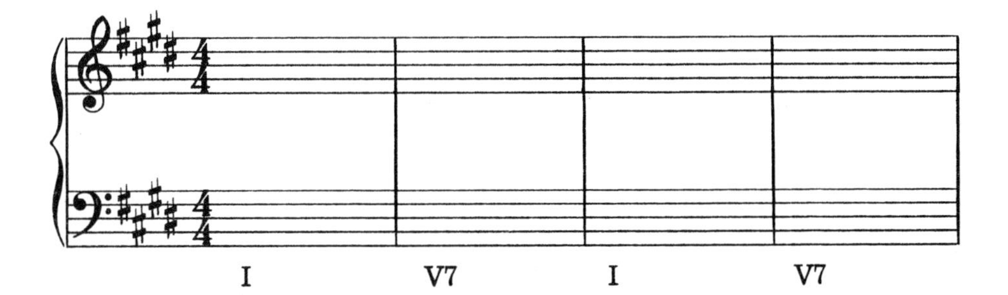
I
V7
I
V7

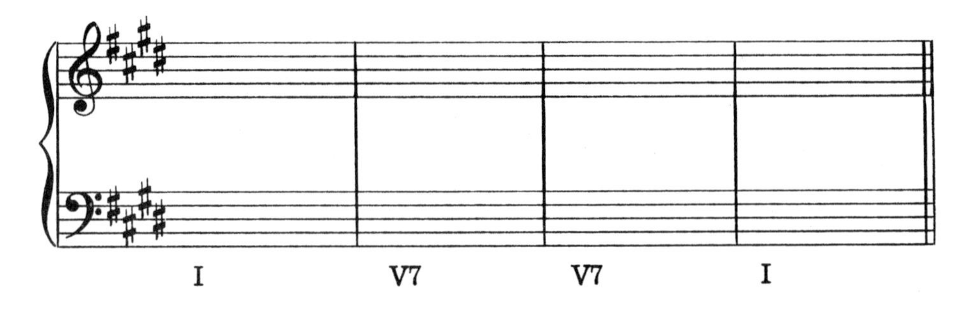
I
V7
V7
I

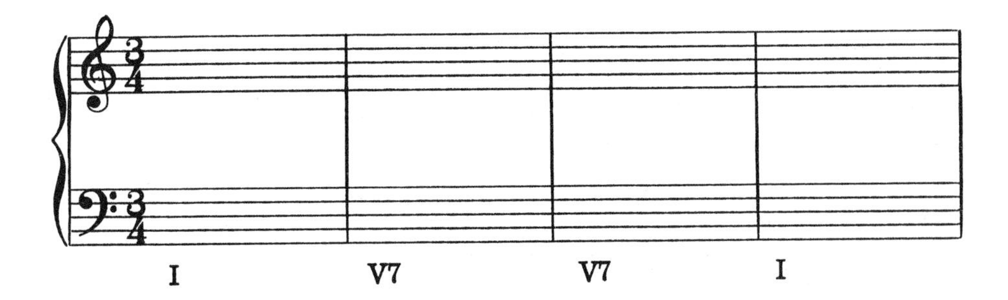
I
V7
V7
I

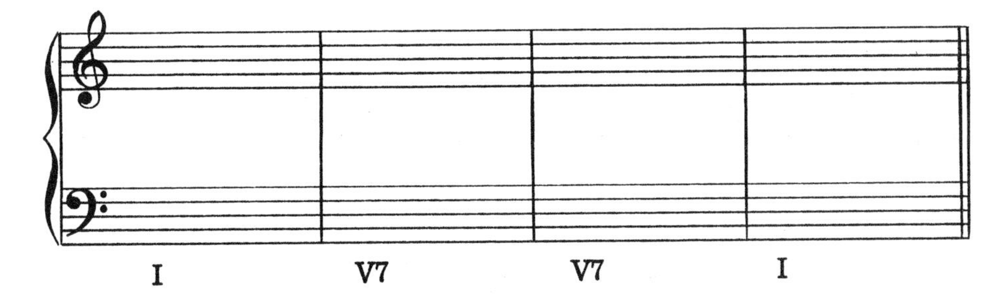
I
V7
V7
I

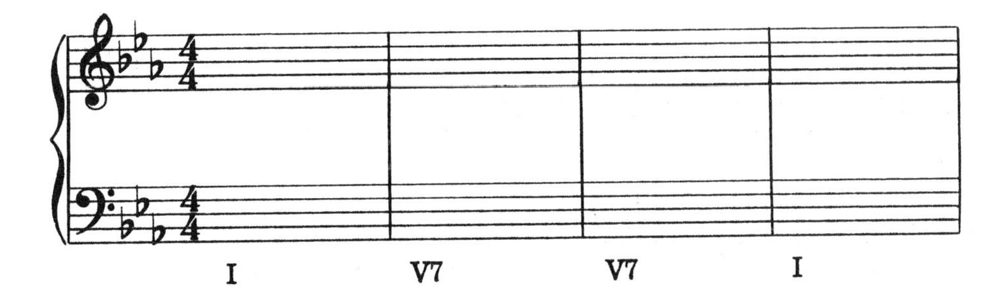
I
V7
V7
I

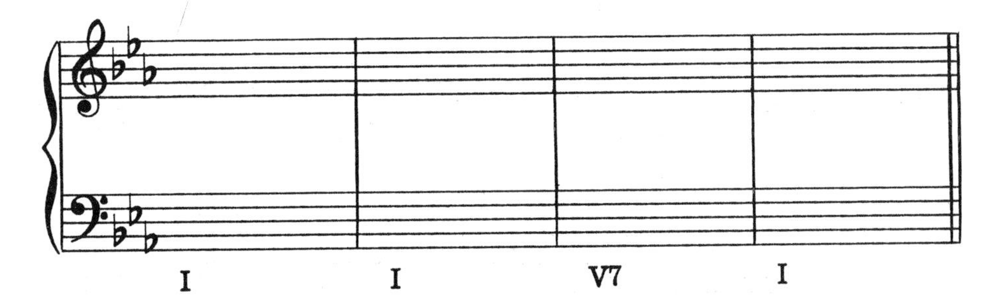
I
I
V7
I

Now write two melodies using passing tones and upper and lower neighbors.

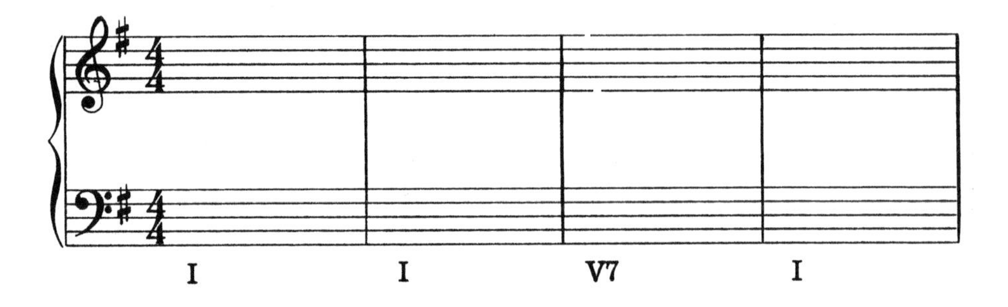

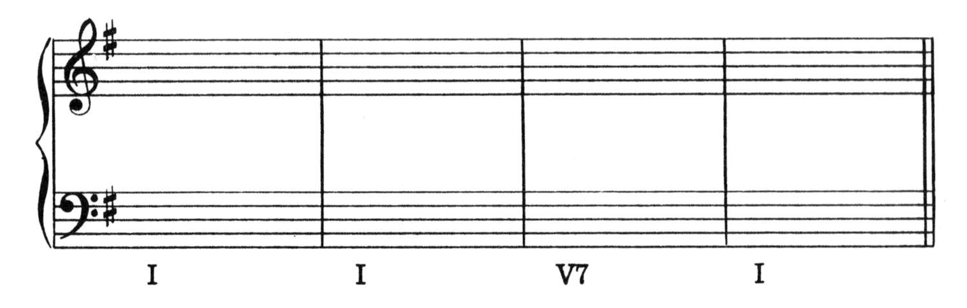

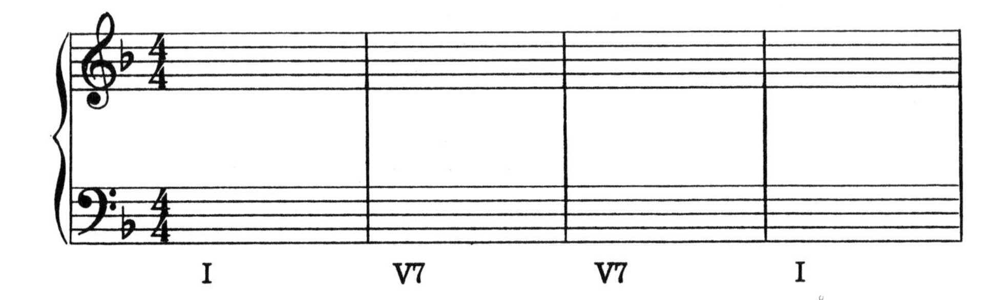

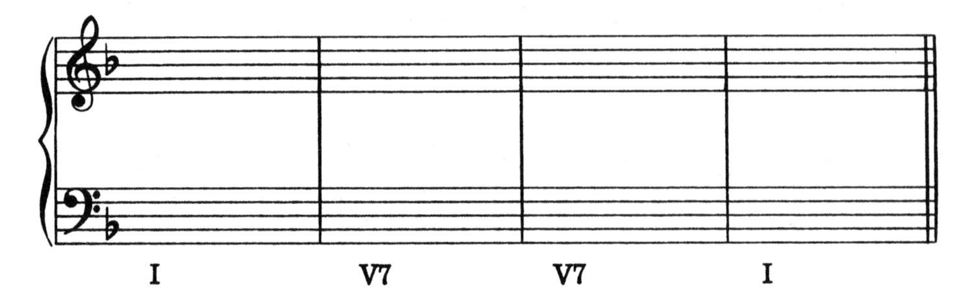

Now select any chord sequence and create a melody of your own. Although measures five to eight may differ from measures one to four, there should be something to relate them, either rhythmically or melodically.

Musical Form

It is important to have some knowledge of phrase structure and cadences in order to understand the basic organization of music. Such organization is called *musical form.*

Let us begin with the *motive*, a small, yet important part of any melody. A *motive* is either a melodic, rhythmic, or harmonic pattern generally no longer than one or two measures. While it does not express a complete musical idea, it does set the distinctive quality of any melody. Here are the motives of some well-known songs:

Motives may either be repeated exactly (called *repetition*) or repeated on a different tone of the scale (called *sequence*).

SILENT NIGHT

repetition

Si - lent night, ho - ly night, All is calm, all is bright.

POLLY WOLLY DOODLE

repetition

Oh, I went down south for to see my Sal, Sing

Pol - ly wol - ly doo- dle all the day.

SHOEMAKER'S DANCE

repetition

SKIP TO MY LOU

sequence

Lou, Lou, skip to my Lou; Lou, Lou, skip to my Lou;

Lou, Lou, skip to my Lou; skip to my Lou my dar - lin'.

BOW, BOW, BELINDA

sequence

Bow, bow, bow, Be-lin-da; Bow, bow, bow, Be-lin-da;

CLEMENTINE

sequence

In a cav- ern, in a can- yon, ex-ca - vat - ing for a mine,

The next larger musical idea is a *phrase*. It is developed from one or more melodic, rhythmic, or harmonic ideas and may require completion by subsequent phrases.

SKIP TO MY LOU

Traditional

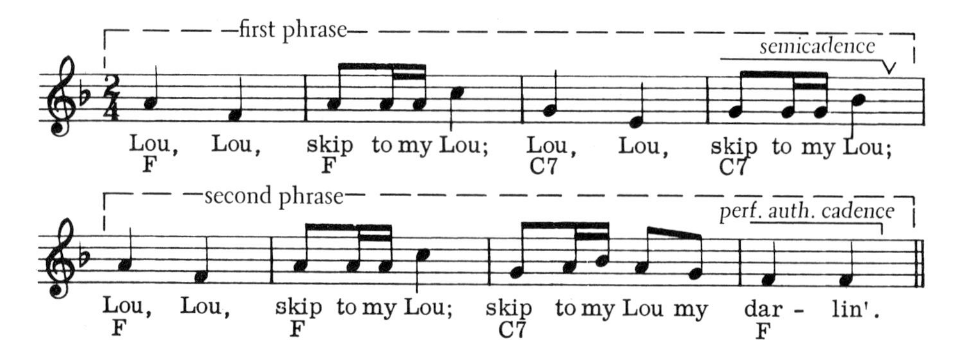

POLLY WOLLY DOODLE

American Song

BOW, BOW, BELINDA

American Game Song

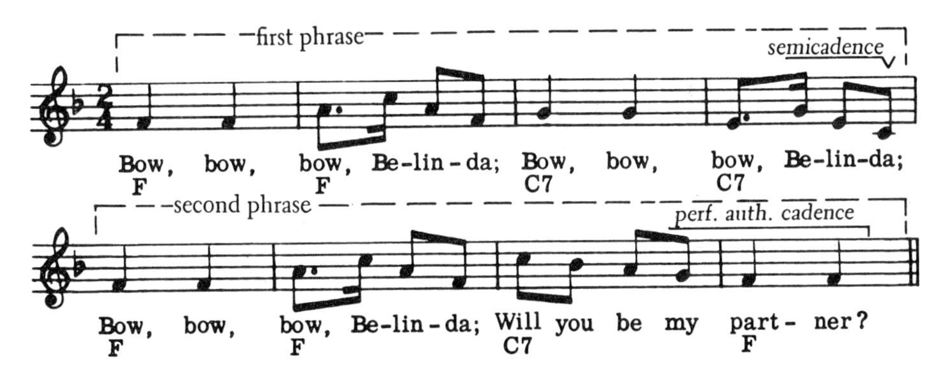

At the end of each of these phrases is a *cadence*, which is a means of musical punctuation. In each example, there is a *semicadence* (I—V_7) in the fourth measure indicated by ——∨ , which gives a slight feeling of rest, but not of completion. A complete or *perfect authentic* cadence (V_7—I) indicated by ——┐ occurs in the eighth measure.[2] Two *phrases* combined, the first having an *incomplete cadence* and the second a *complete cadence*, make a *period*.[3]

When both phrases begin with the same motive, they form a *parallel* period, as in the case of "Bow, Bow, Belinda" and "Skip to My Lou." A *contrasting* period results when the motive of the second phrase differs from the first, as in "Clementine."

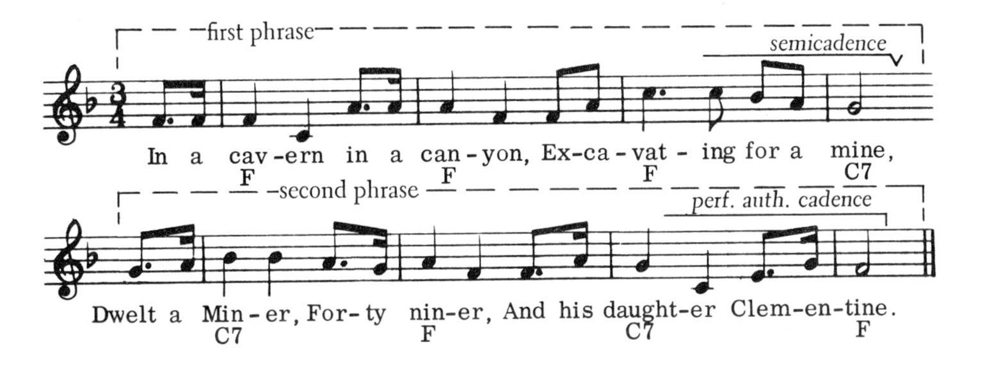

[2] In the perfect authentic cadence, the key tone of the I chord must always be the top note (soprano). If the third or fifth note of the chord is the top note, it is called an *imperfect authentic cadence* (——\ ).

[3] Do not confuse the curved line phrase marking ⌒ (see page 33) with the symbols for the cadence at the end of a phrase (——∨ or ——┐). For a complete list of cadence symbols, see Appendix B.

1. Fill in the key signatures and the I and V_7 chords in both forms as shown here.

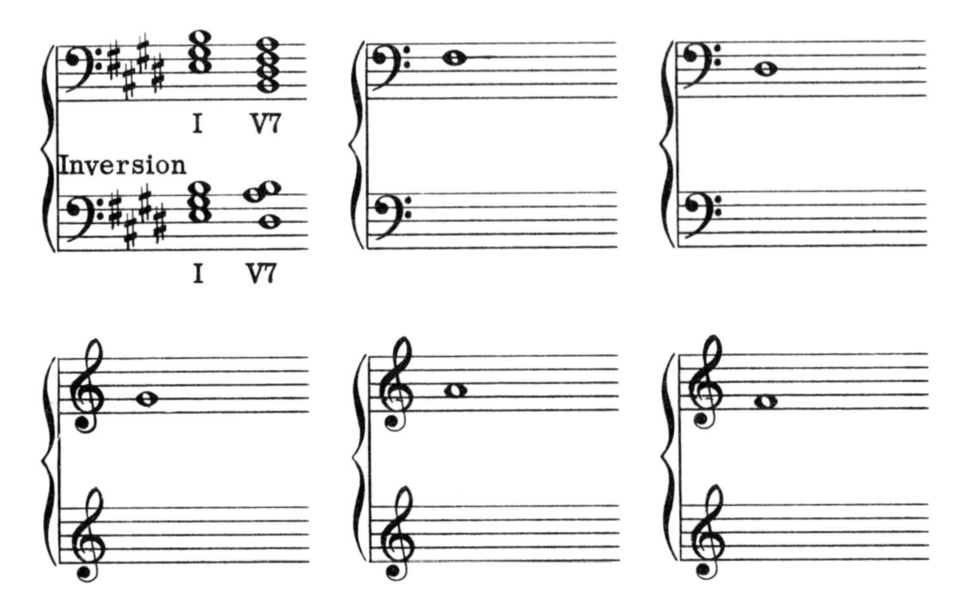

2. Accompany yourself with the I and V_7 chords on the Autoharp or piano as you sing the following songs. Use this position on the piano, in the proper key.

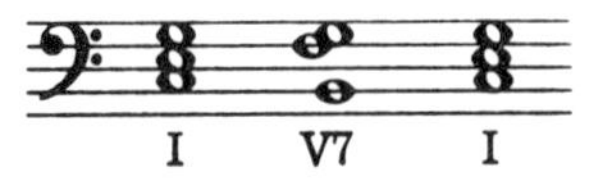

THE FARMER IN THE DELL

Singing Game

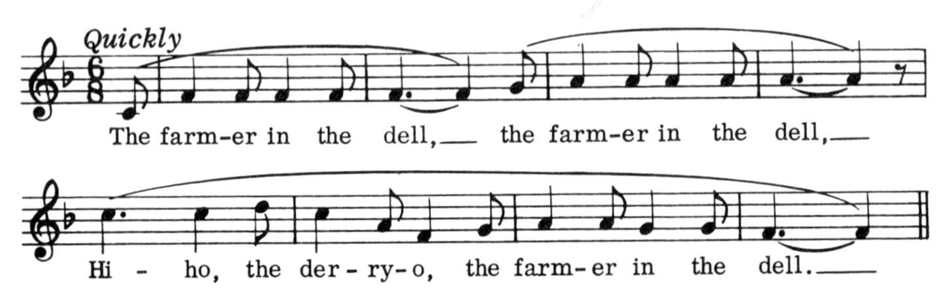

BRIDGE OF AVIGNON

French Folk Song

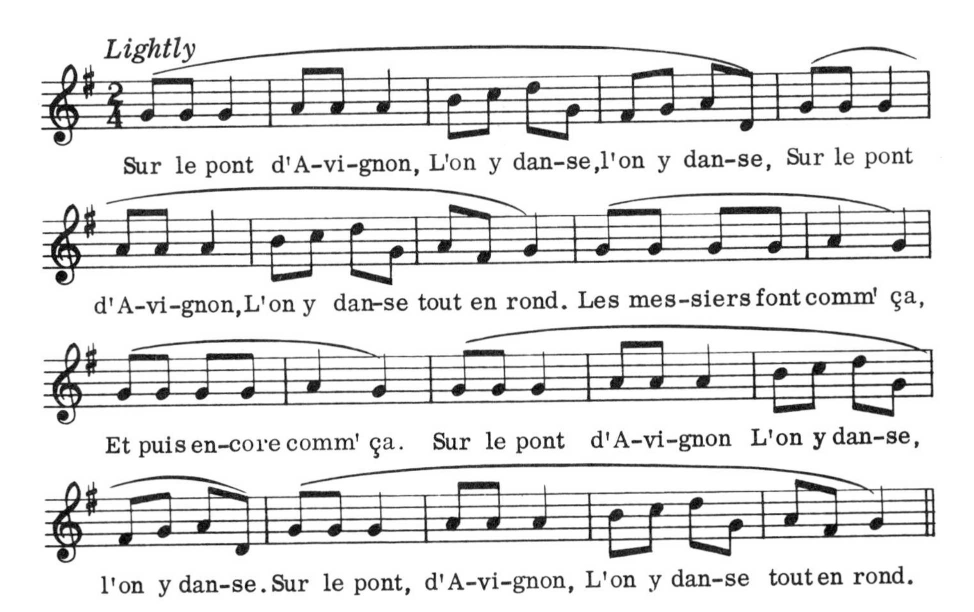

DOWN IN THE VALLEY

American Folk Song

LONG, LONG AGO

Thomas Haynes Bayley

3. Circle all chord tones in these melodies.

American Folk Song

ROSA

Flemish Folk Song

4. Label all non-chord tones in these melodies: upper neighbor (UN); lower neighbor (LN); passing tone (PT).

LONDON BRIDGE

Traditional

WHERE, OH WHERE HAS MY LITTLE DOG GONE?

Traditional

5. Write chord-tone melodies for these chord progressions. First establish your rhythm and meter, then improvise your melody.

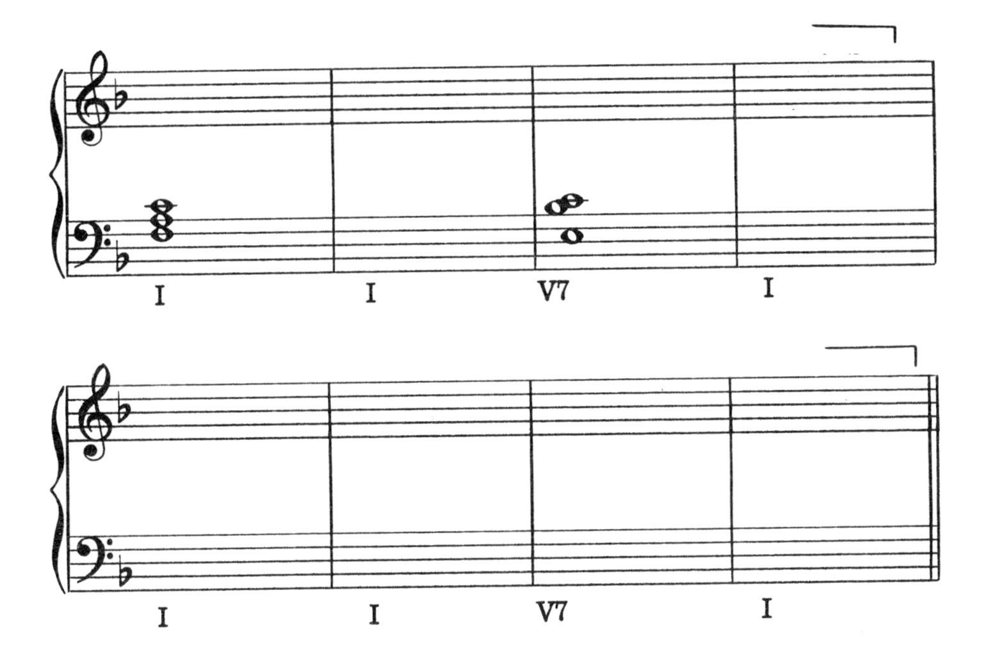

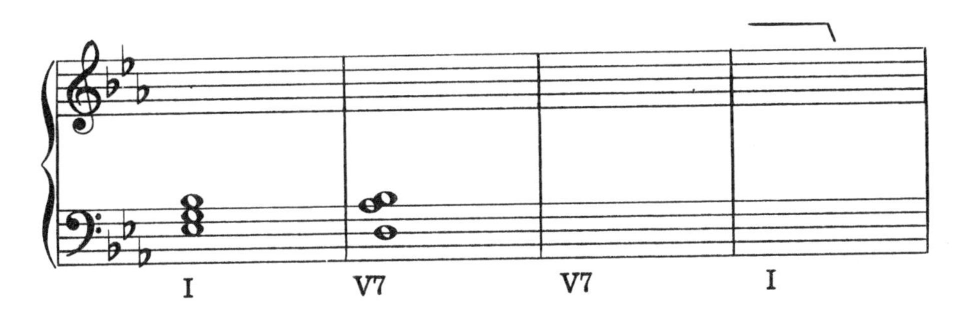

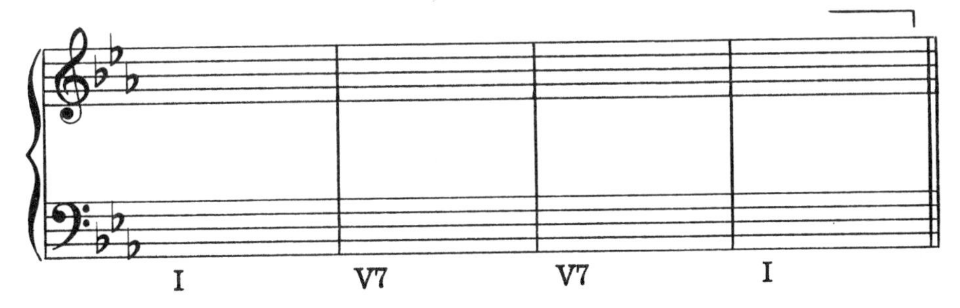

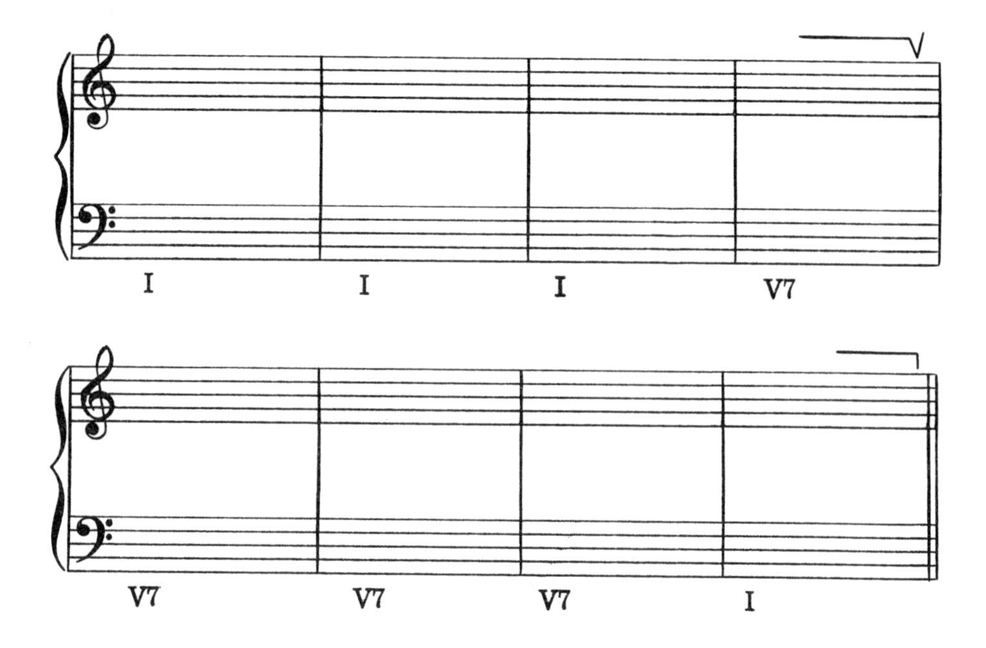

6. Write melodies for the same progressions as in 5, now using passing tones and upper and lower neighbors.

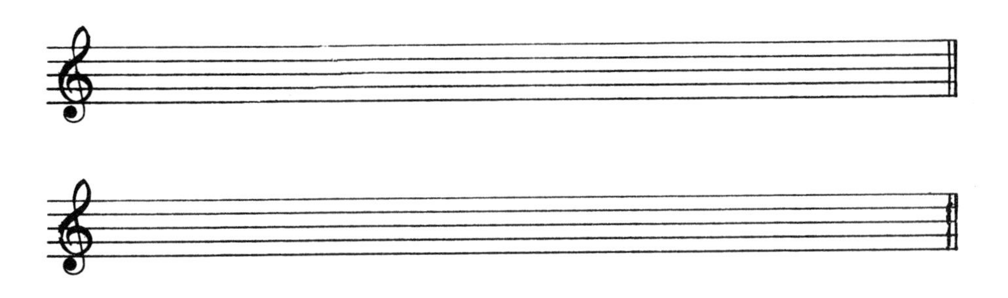

7. Mark the repetitions in these melodies.

THE CAMPBELLS ARE COMING

Robert Burns

Scottish Folk Song

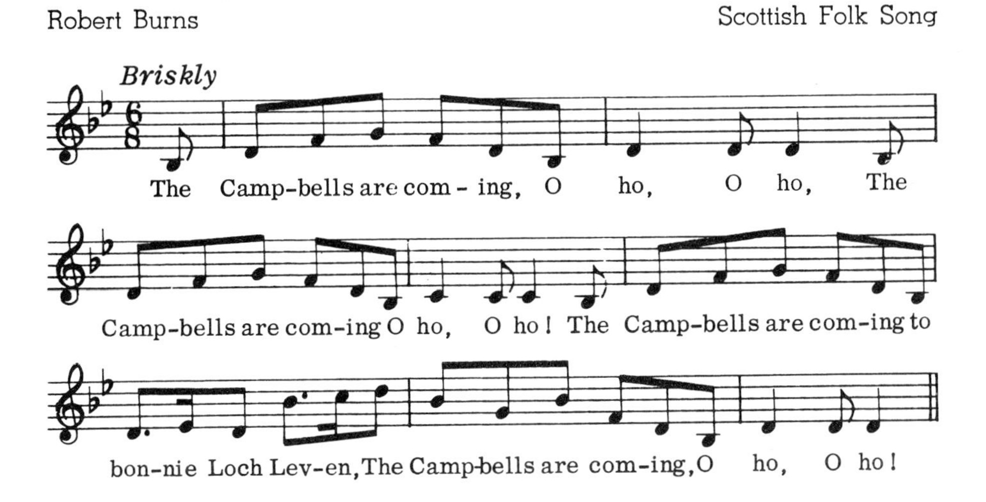

SHOO FLY

American Singing Game

ALL THROUGH THE NIGHT

H. Boulton

Old Welsh Air

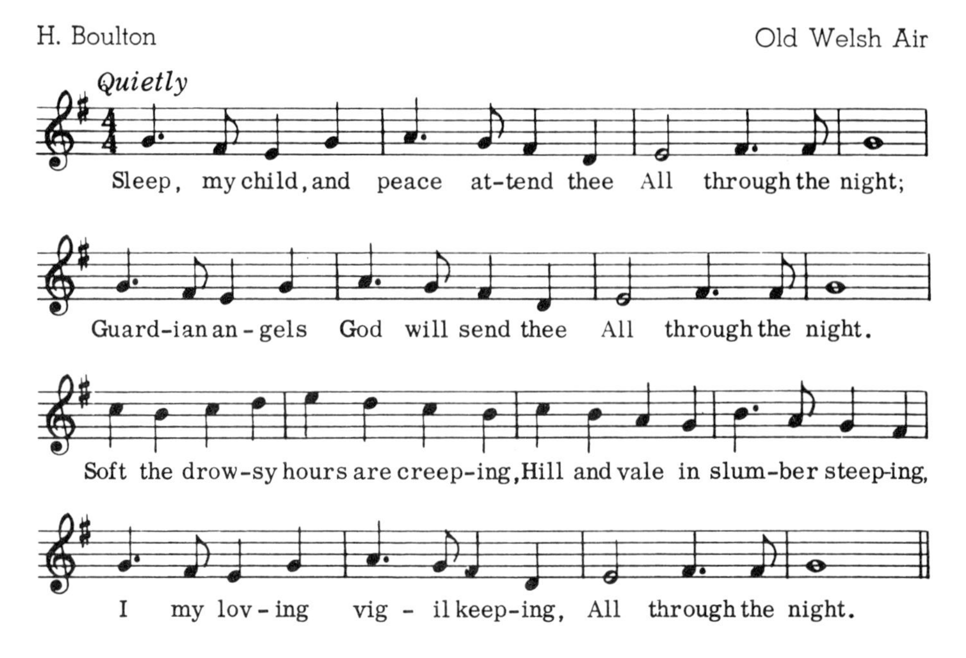

8. Mark the sequences (⌐¬) in these melodies.

COCKLES AND MUSSELS

English Folk Song

BUFFALO GALS

Cool White

9. Identify parallel or contrasting periods.

OH SUSANNA

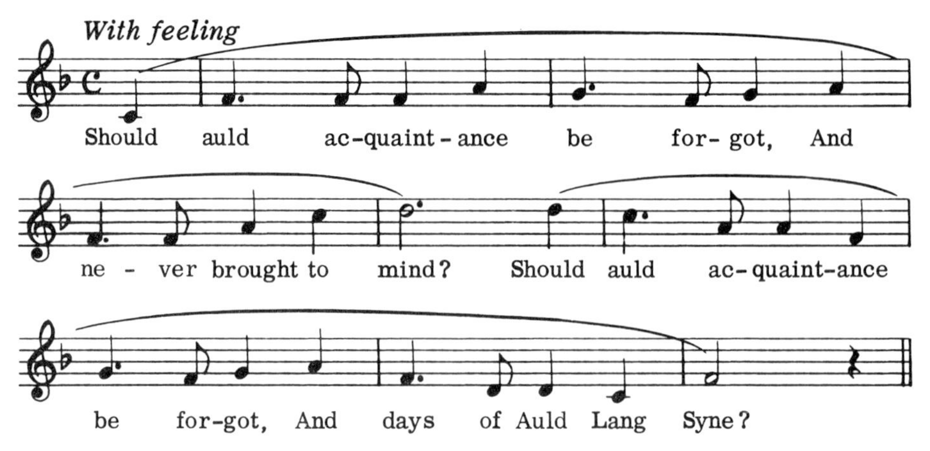
With feeling
Should auld ac-quaint-ance be for- got, And
ne - ver brought to mind? Should auld ac- quaint-ance
be for-got, And days of Auld Lang Syne?

3

The I, IV, and V_7 Chords

As you have observed, there are numerous songs that can be harmonized with only the I and V_7 chords. However, you will soon find that there are many songs that require still another chord. For example, try to harmonize "Jimmie Crack Corn" with the I and V_7 chords only.

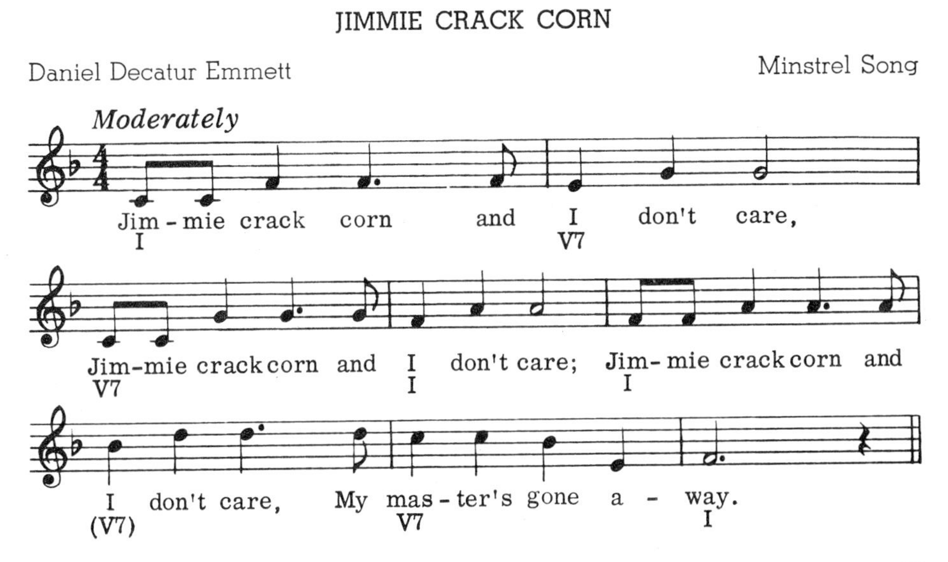

Neither of these chords is quite satisfactory for the sixth measure. To harmonize the melody in this measure you need the IV or *subdominant* chord. Like the I and V_7 chords, it takes its name from the degree of the scale on which the root of the chord is found.

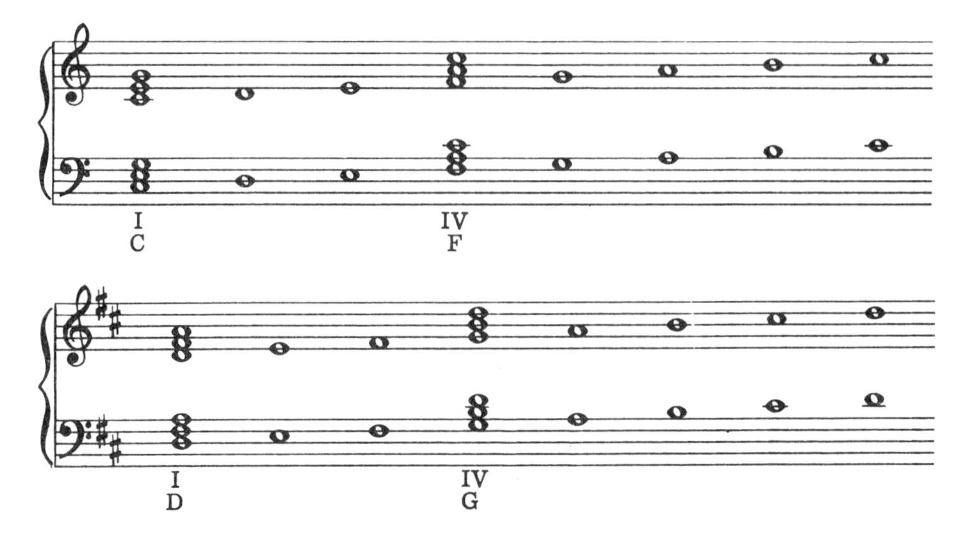

In the key of C, play the C major (I) and F major (IV) chords on the Autoharp until you are familiar with the sound of these two chords. While it is not possible to play the I and IV chord of every key on the Autoharp, it is easy to play them on the piano. This inversion of the IV chord is commonly used:[1]

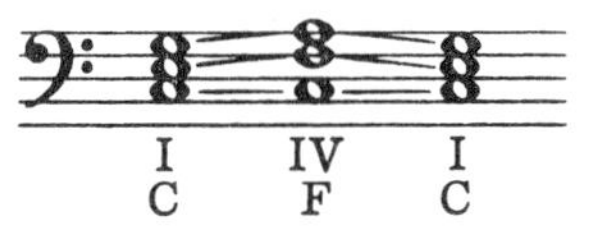

To play the I—IV—I chord progression in any key, remember that:

a. The top note always moves *up one whole step.*
b. The middle note always moves *up one half step.*
c. The bottom note *remains the same.*

Play the I—IV—I progression in these keys:

---

[1] Technically, this is the IV^6_4 chord. For simplicity, however, we shall refer to it as a IV chord without giving the subscript.

When the IV—I progression occurs at the end of a song it is known as a *plagal cadence*. It is most frequently found at the end of hymns and is our second type of *complete cadence*.

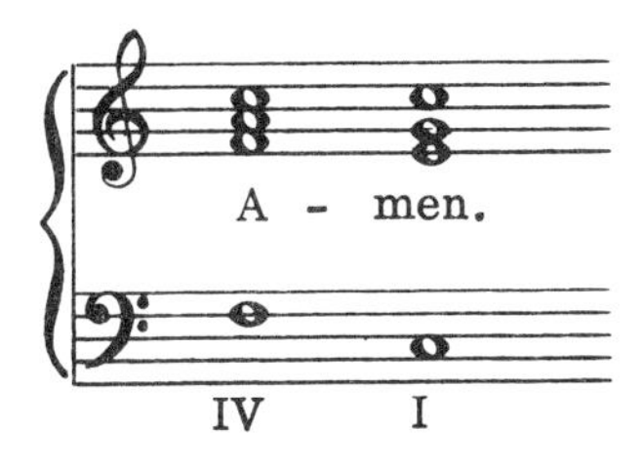

Next, try this chord progression on the Autoharp or piano:

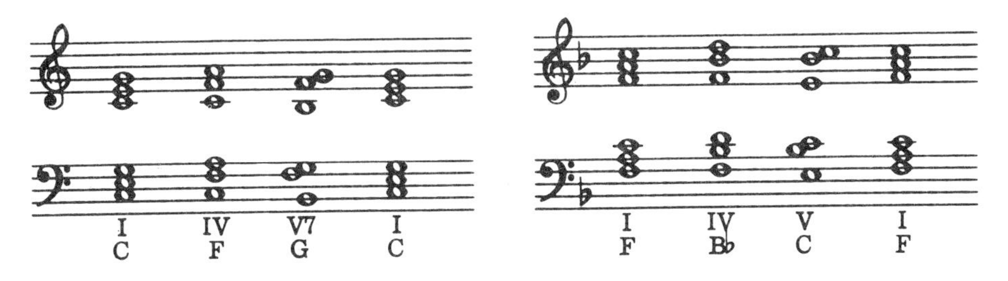

Sing these songs and harmonize them with the I, IV, and V_7 chords, using either the Autoharp or the piano. Write the number of the chord you would use.

GOOD NIGHT, LADIES

College Song

RED RIVER VALLEY

American Folk Song

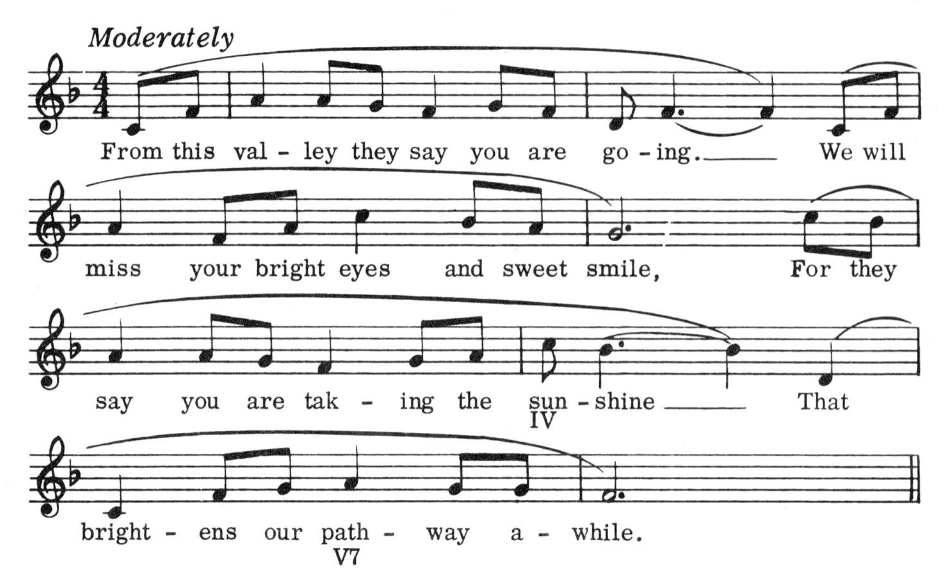

Chord Tones

Recognizing chord tones in a melody not only facilitates sight-reading, but also simplifies the process of harmonizing songs. Remember that the tones in the harmony must be related to the tones in the melody.

Circle the chord tones in these melodies:

HOME ON THE RANGE

Dr. Brewster Higley

Dan Kelly

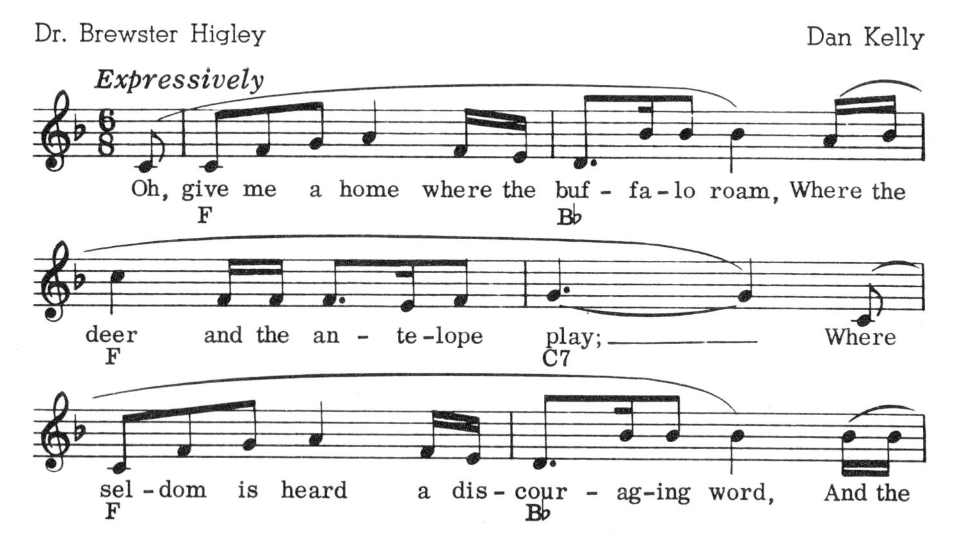

O WORSHIP THE KING

J. Michael Haydn

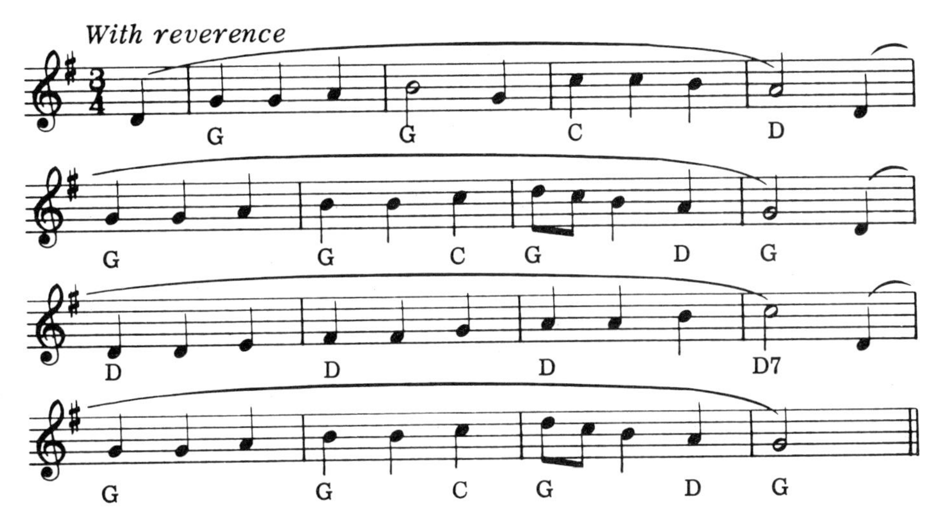

I COULDN'T HEAR NOBODY PRAY

Negro Spiritual

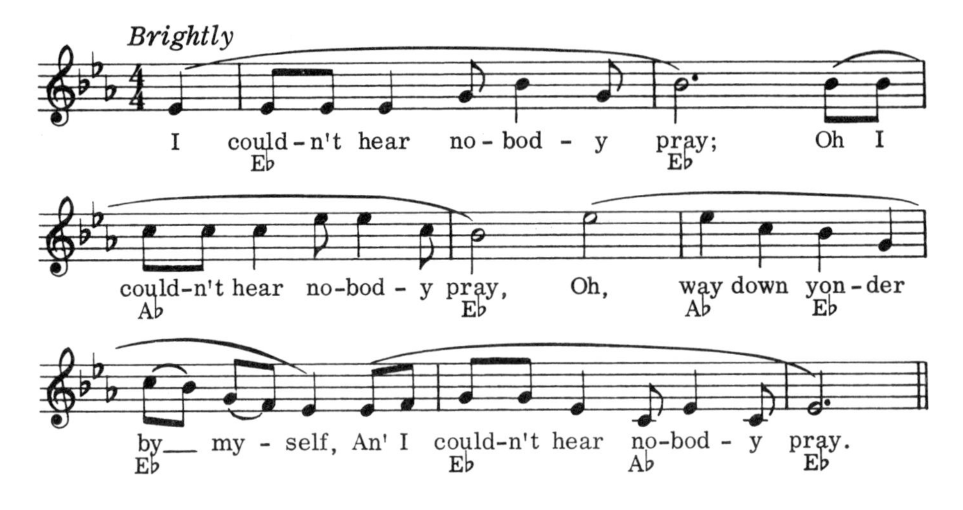

Improvising Melodies with the I, IV, and V_7 Chords

Here is a chord pattern for a parallel period. Create your own melodies for parallel periods, as in the example, using only chord tones from the I, IV, and V_7 chords.

Example:

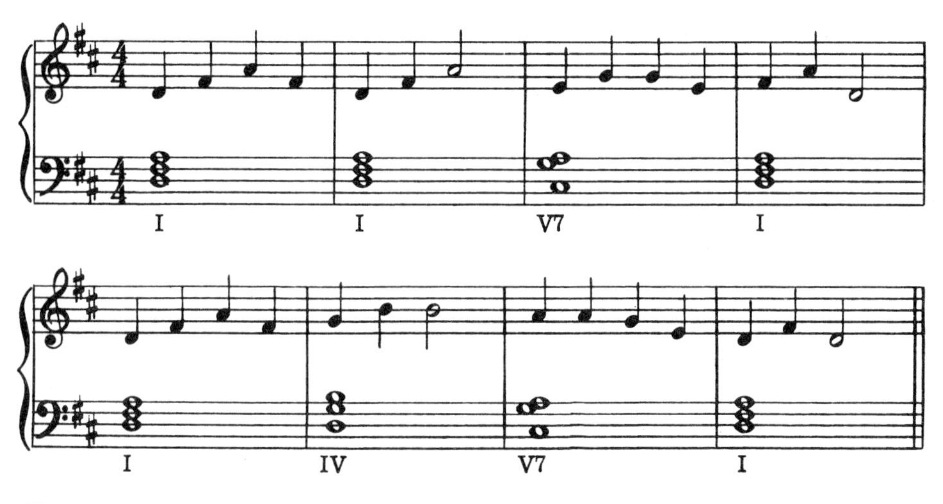

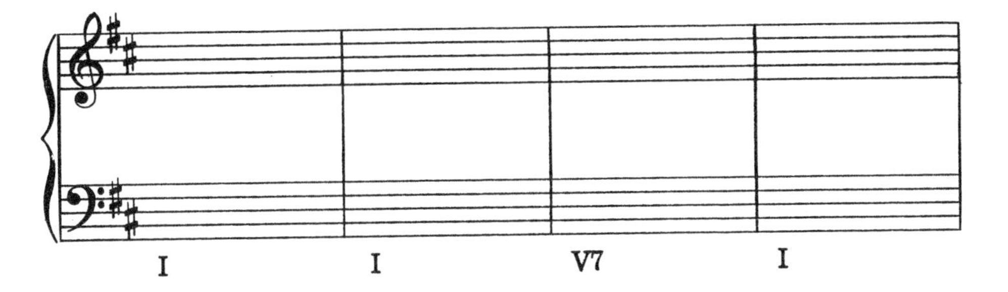
I
I
V7
I

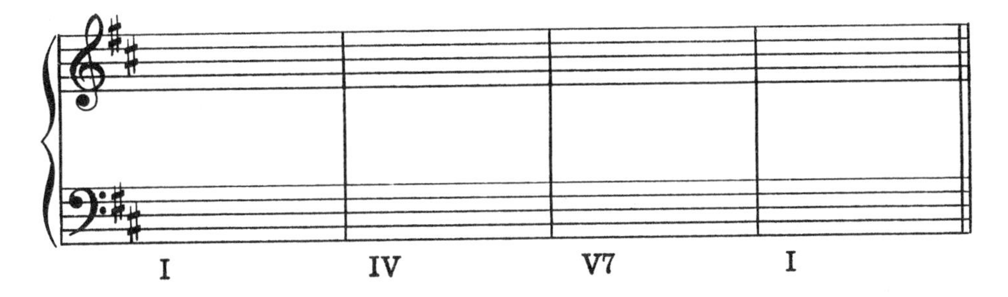
I
IV
V7
I

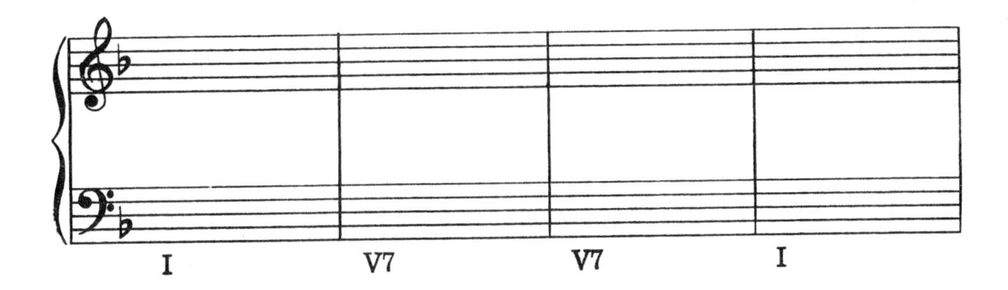
I
V7
V7
I

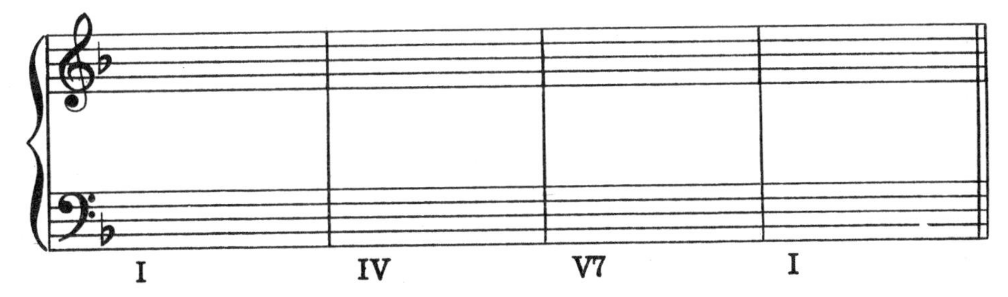
I
IV
V7
I

Using these same chord progressions, make up new melodies, this time with passing tones and upper and lower neighbors, as well as chord tones.

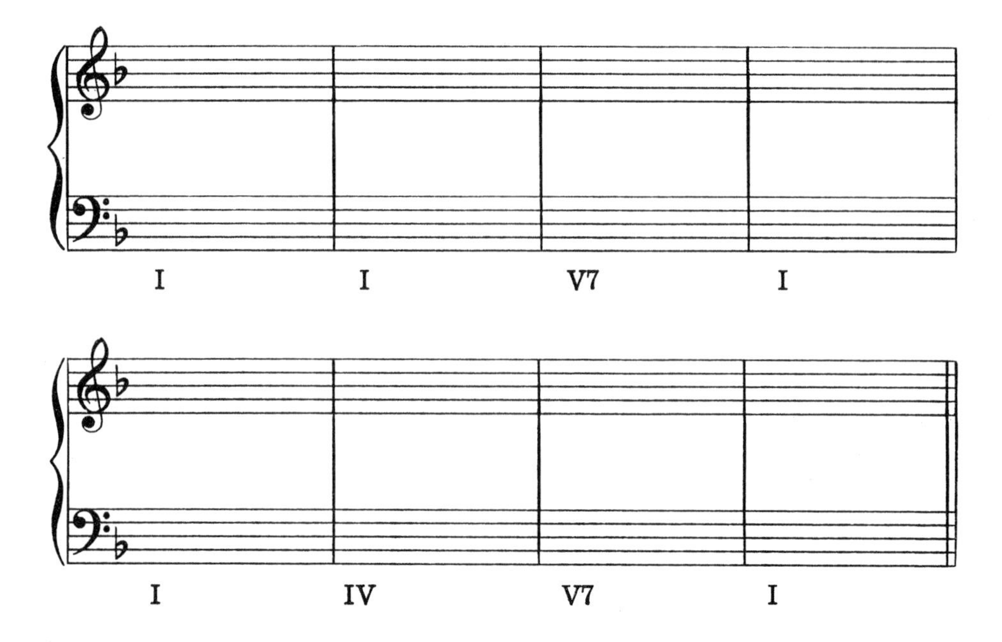

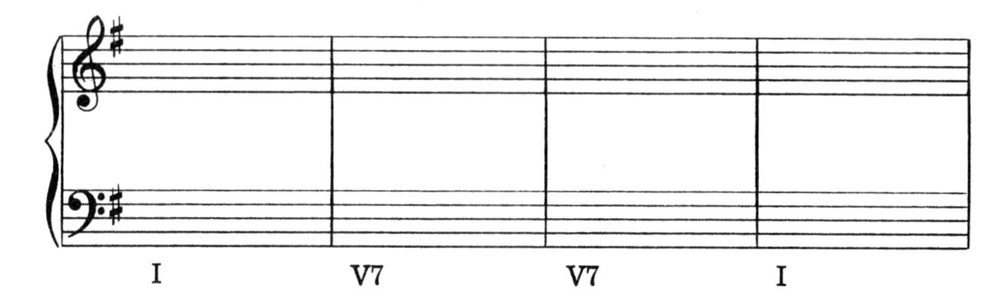

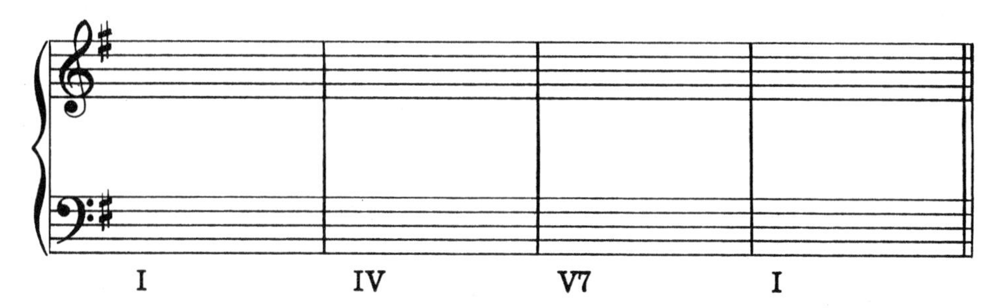

Primary Units of Form

Most songs can be divided into several short sections of similar length. Each section will represent one of the four primary units of form: phrase (see page 42), period (page 43), double period, and phrase group.

Just as the period is made up of two phrases, the *double period* is made up of four phrases (generally sixteen measures), with a semicadence in the middle and a complete cadence at the end only. The double period may also be parallel or contrasting, as was the period.

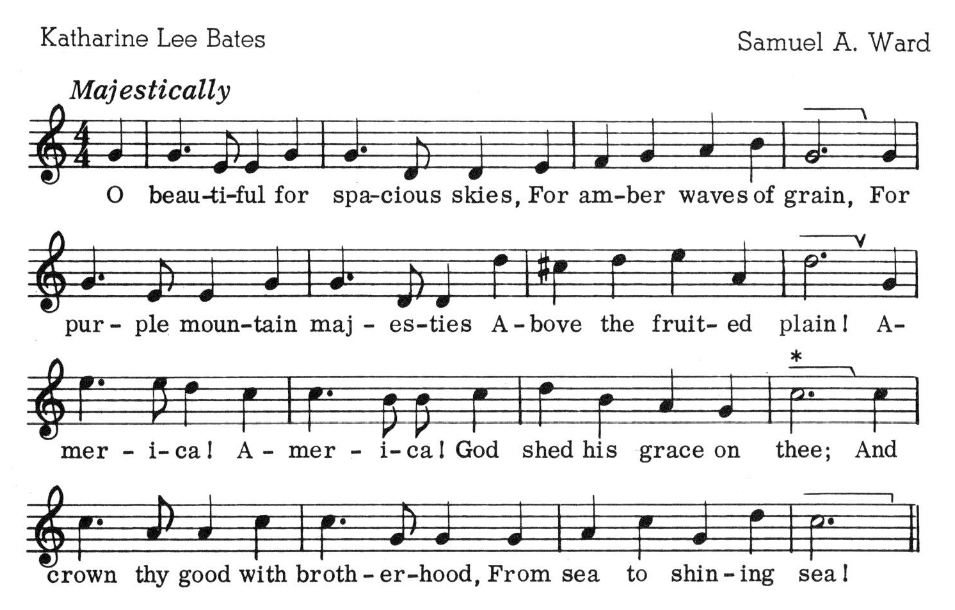

The *phrase group*, a substitute for the *period* form, is generally composed of three phrases, each of which is slightly different. Only the last phrase ends with a *complete* cadence, the others being *incomplete*. For example, "Silent Night" has three phrases, each one slightly different from the other.

---

* In this context, the V to the I chord gives the feeling of an incomplete cadence.

SILENT NIGHT

Joseph Mohr — Franz Gruber

Any one of these units (phrase, period, double period, or phrase group), when considered separately, is a *one-part form*. For example, "Up, Little Hans" is a one-part form consisting of a parallel period.

UP, LITTLE HANS

Scandinavian Folk Song

When combined, the units result in *two-*, *three-*, or *five-part forms*, called *song forms*. "Yankee Doodle" is made up of two parallel periods. Therefore it is a *two-part song form*, the respective periods being designated as A and B.

YANKEE DOODLE

Traditional American

Song literature abounds with examples of the *three-part form* (A B A), such as "The More We Get Together."

THE MORE WE GET TOGETHER

German Folk Song

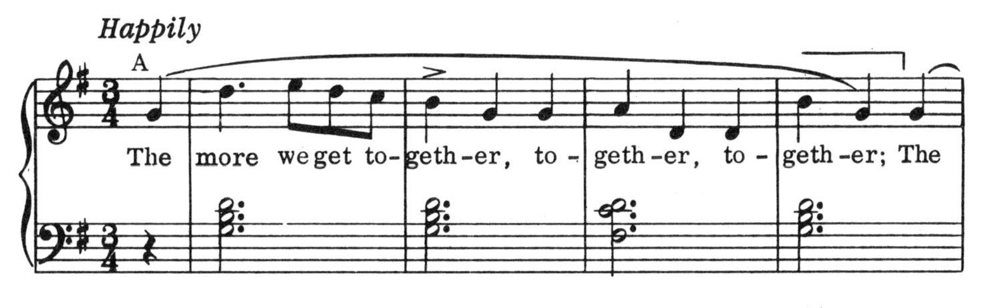

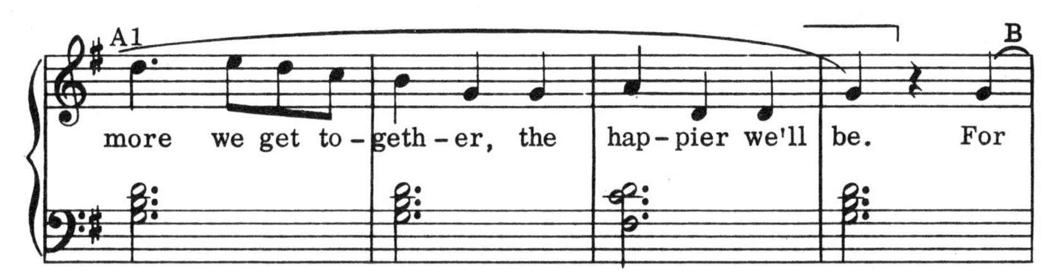

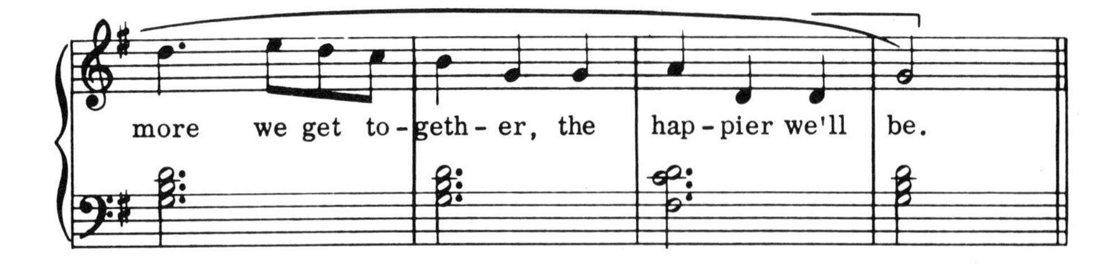

Part I (A) ends with a complete cadence. The melodic material of Part II (B) may or may not be directly related to Part I. In this case it is derived from the third and fourth measures of Part I. It ends with an incomplete cadence and is immediately followed by Part III (A_1) which is a restatement of material from Part I. Frequently, as in "The More We Get Together," Part III is abbreviated, although it can be a complete restatement as in "Oh Dear, What Can the Matter Be?"

OH DEAR, WHAT CAN THE MATTER BE?

Old English Song

Plaintively, but not too slowly

FOR FURTHER STUDY

1. Fill in the I—IV—V_7—I chords.

Example:

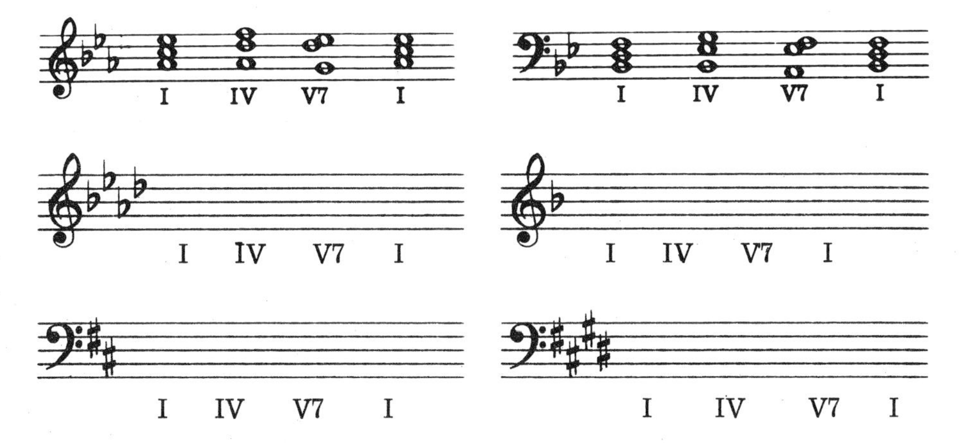

2. Accompany yourself with the I—IV—V_7 chords on the Autoharp or piano as you sing these songs.

THE FLY AND THE BUMBLEBEE

English Folk Song

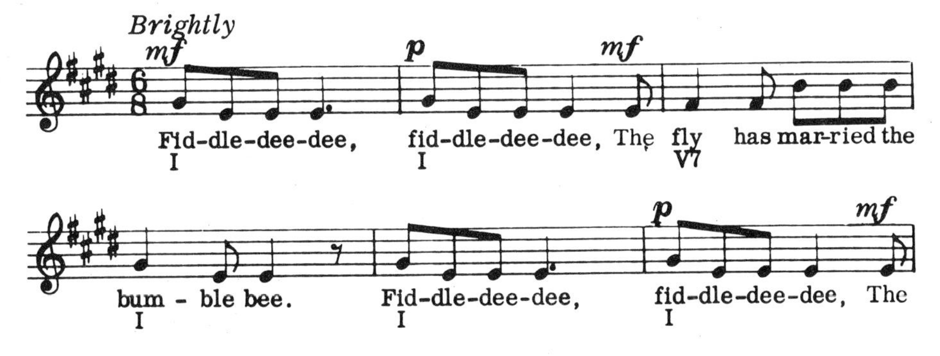

TWINKLE, TWINKLE, LITTLE STAR

Nursery Song

THE BARNYARD

American Song

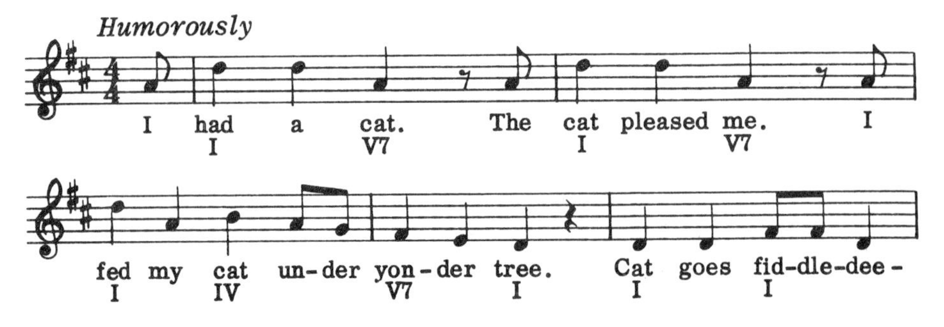

3. Circle all chord tones in these melodies.

STODOLA-PUMPA

Czecho-Slovakian Folk Song

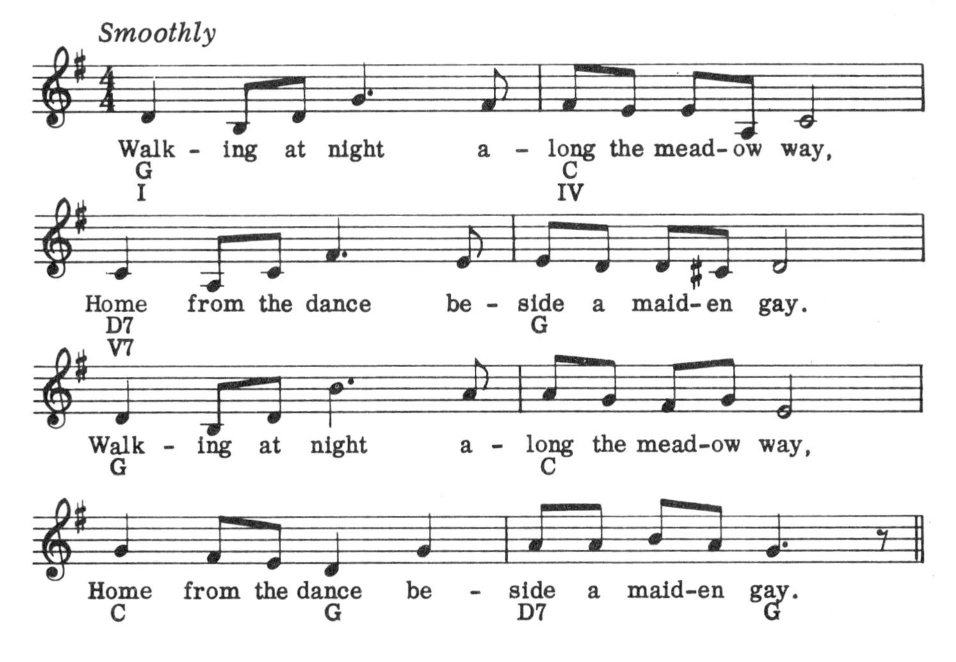

PAPER OF PINS

Traditional

4. Label all the non-chord tones in this melody.

5. Write chord-tone melodies for these chord progressions, which are parallel periods.

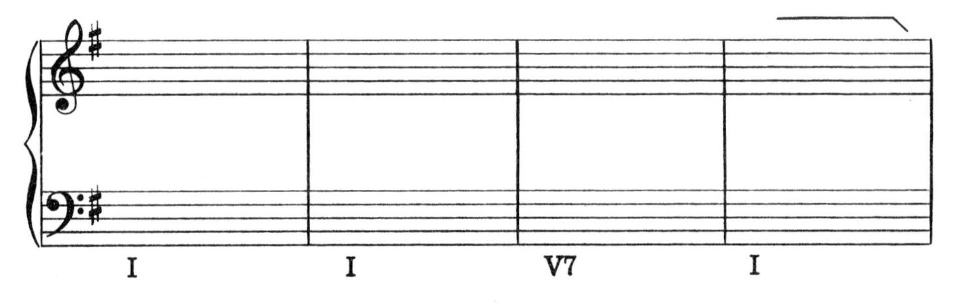

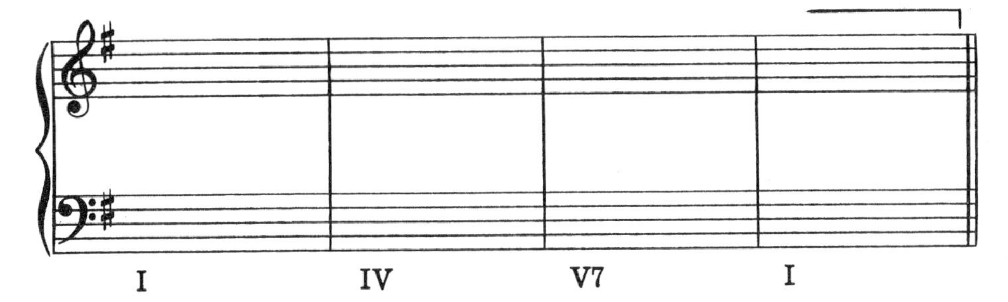

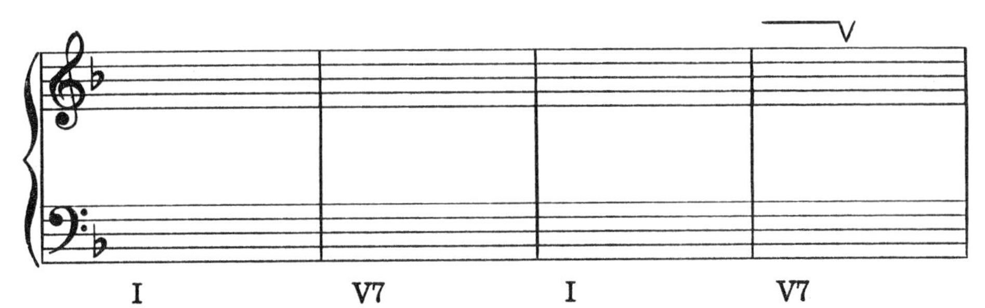

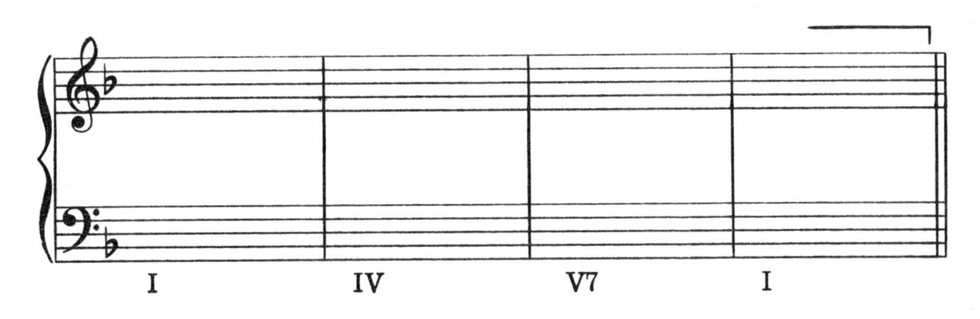

6. Write melodies for the same progressions as in No. 5 using passing tones and upper and lower neighbors.

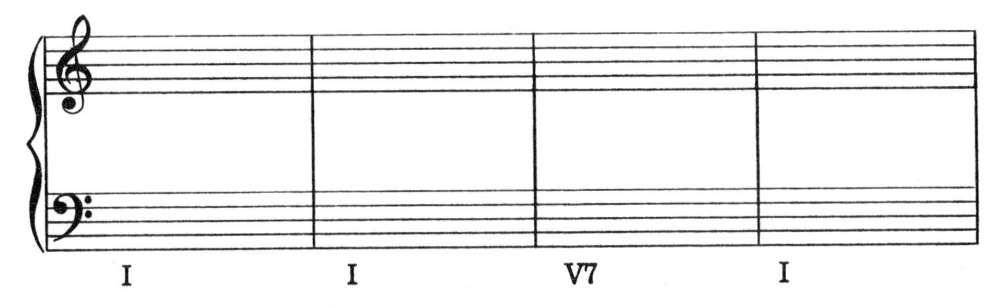

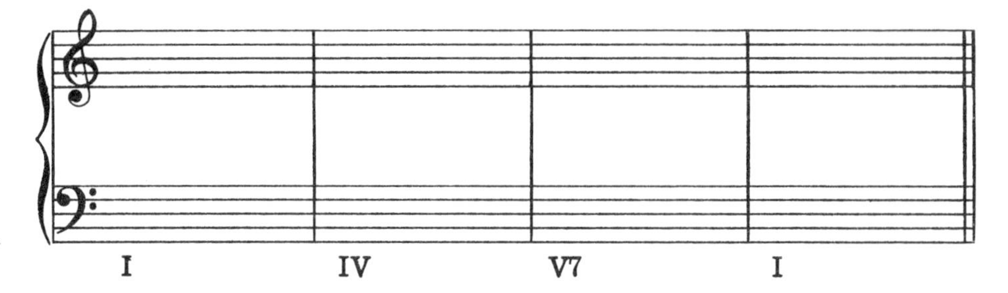

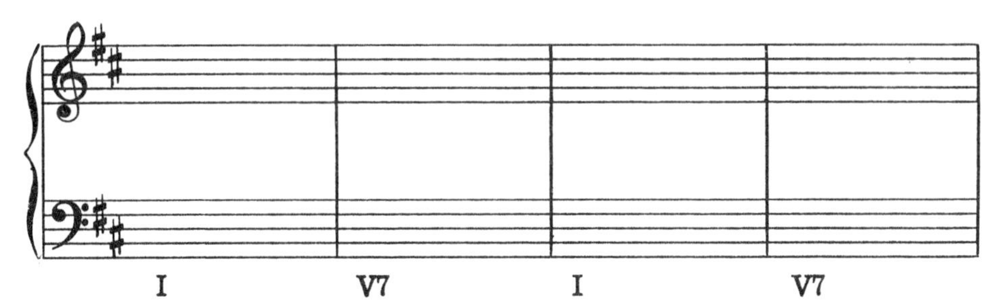

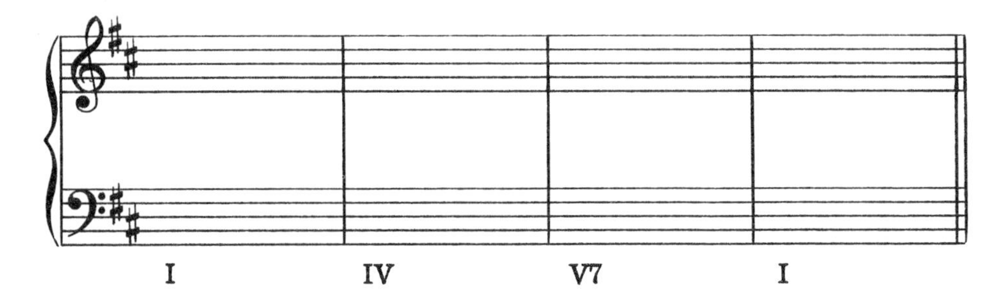

7. Identify repeated phrases, periods, double periods, or phrase groups in the following songs:

DRINK TO ME ONLY WITH THINE EYES

BARBARA ALLEN

FLOW GENTLY, SWEET AFTON

* Fermata—to hold slightly longer.

RED RIVER VALLEY

8. State whether each of the following is a one-, two-, or three-part song form.

ALOUETTE

French Folk Song

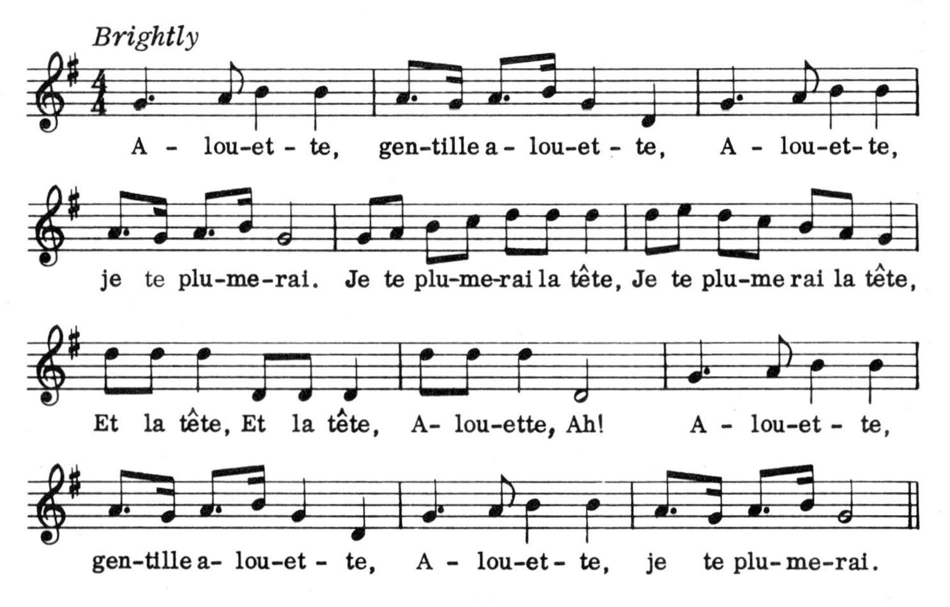

AU CLAIR DE LA LUNE

French Folk Song

CLEMENTINE

American Folk Song

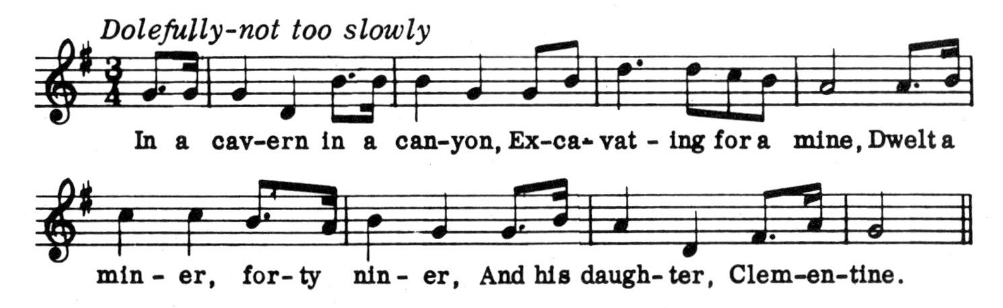

BATTLE HYMN OF THE REPUBLIC

9. Improvise a two-part song form and provide the chord background for Autoharp or piano.

10. Improvise a three-part song form and provide the chord background for Autoharp or piano.

4

Minor Chords and Minor Keys

Let us review the chords built on the first, fourth, and fifth degrees of the C major scale. As you will recall, all chord intervals are counted upward from the bottom tone.

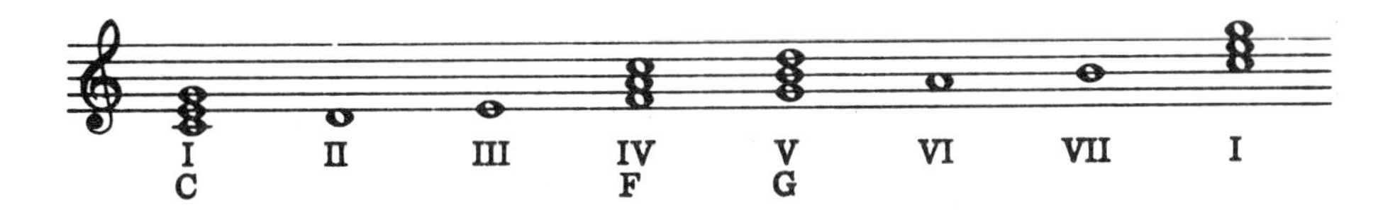

Play the tones of the I, IV, and V chords (not V_7) on the melody bells or piano. You will notice that each chord is composed of a *major 3rd* (two whole steps) on the bottom and a *perfect 5th* from the bottom note to the top. These are *major triads* (three-tone chords).

Now play the tones of the II, III, and VI chords of the C major scale on the melody bells or piano. Each of these chords has a *minor 3rd* (one and a half steps) on the bottom and a *perfect 5th* from the bottom to the top note. These are called *minor triads.*

In summarizing our discussion of chords, we can say that in any major scale the I, IV, and V chords are major and the II, III, and VI chords are minor. The VII chord is *diminished,* since it is composed of a minor 3rd and a diminished 5th.

A major triad becomes minor when the 3rd (middle tone) is *lowered* one half step.

Conversely, a minor triad becomes major when the 3rd is *raised* one half step.

Many songs written in a major key use not only the I, IV, and V chords, but also the II, VI, and sometimes the III chords. Two well-known examples are "America" and the "Doxology."

AMERICA

Samuel F. Smith

Henry Carey

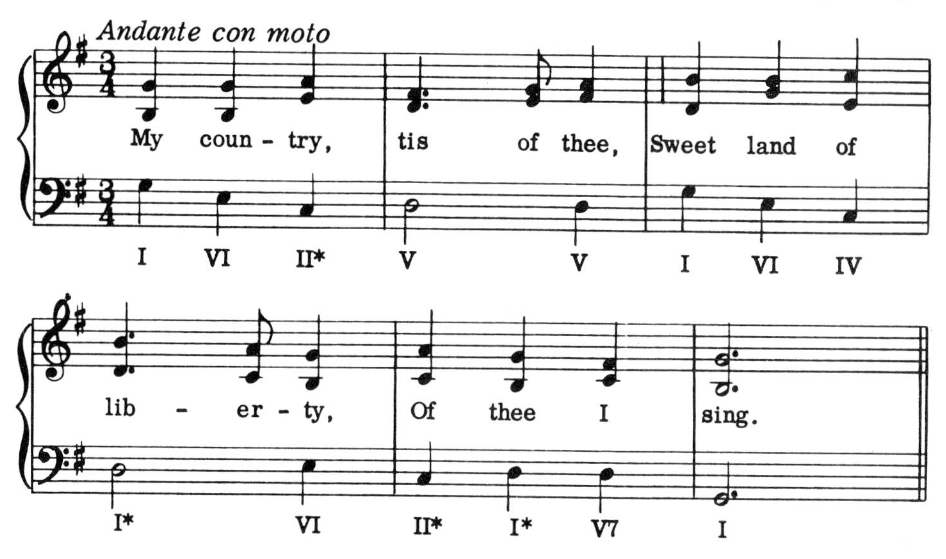

DOXOLOGY

Louis Bourgeois

* These are inversions of the chord.

Relative and Parallel Minor Scales and Keys

The same arrangement of sharps and flats is used in key signatures for both major and minor keys. For every major key there is a *relative minor key*. A relative minor key has the same number of sharps or flats as the major key, which begins a minor 3rd above it. For example, D minor is the relative minor of F major, E minor is the relative minor of G major, etc. The carol "We Three Kings" begins in minor and goes to the relative major in the refrain. (For a complete table of major and minor key signatures, see Appendix A.)

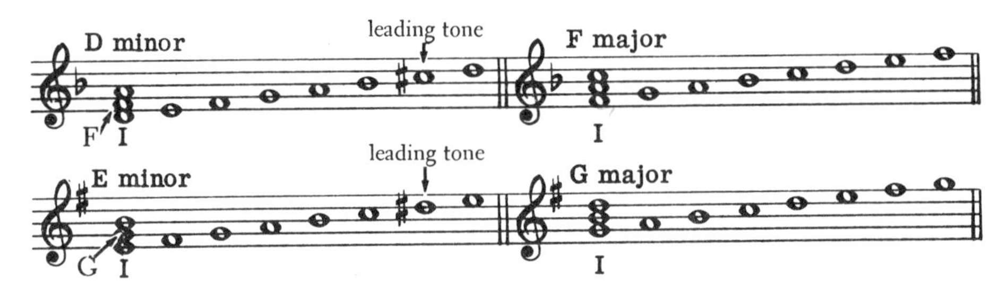

In the above examples, notice that the seventh degree of the scale, or *leading tone*, is raised one half step in minor. Play the examples on bells or piano.

Those major and minor scales that share the *same* keynote are called *parallel keys*.

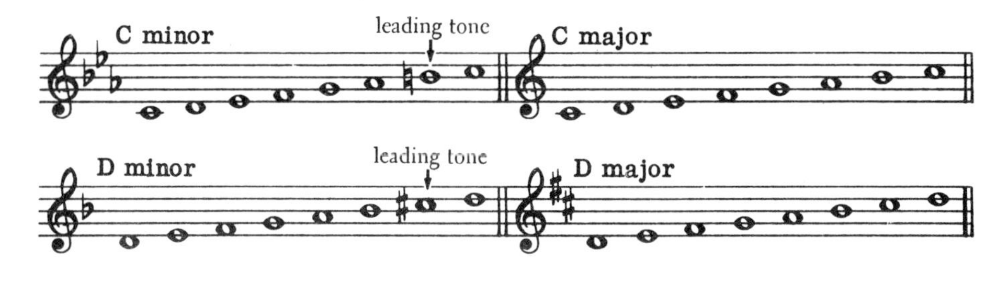

Therefore, C minor is the *parallel minor* of C major, D minor is the *parallel minor* of D major, etc. Notice that *parallel* major and minor keys do *not* have the same key signatures, but have the same tonic or key tone.

A quick check of the first and last chords of a song, as well as its key signature, will help establish whether it is in major or minor mode.

Songs such as "America" and the "Doxology," although they contain some minor chords, are actually in *major mode*. Some of our most expressive music is written in minor mode, however.

JOSHUA FIT DE BATTLE OF JERICHO

American Spiritual

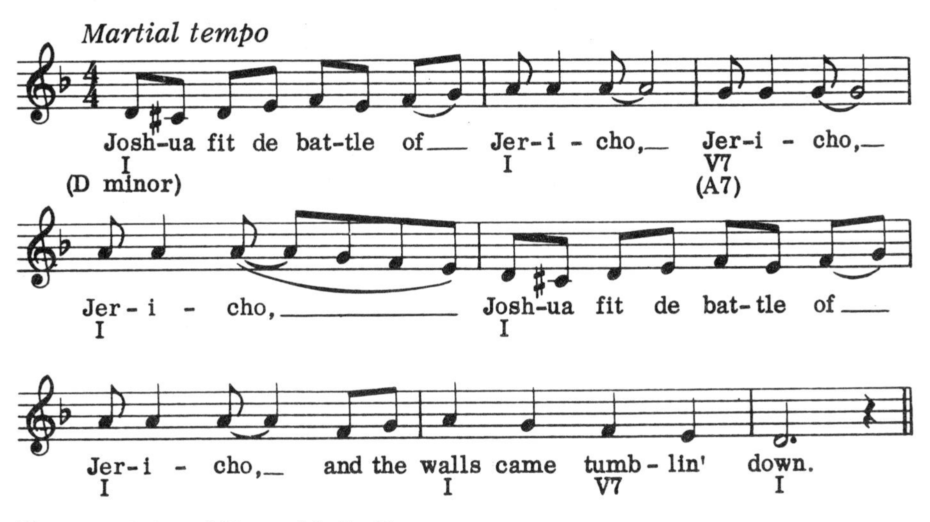

Harmonizing Minor Melodies

In harmonizing minor melodies, notice that the I and IV chords are changed to minor, while the V_7 remains the same as in the parallel major scale.

Harmonize the places indicated by × with the I, IV, and V_7 chords.

OLD KING COLE

English

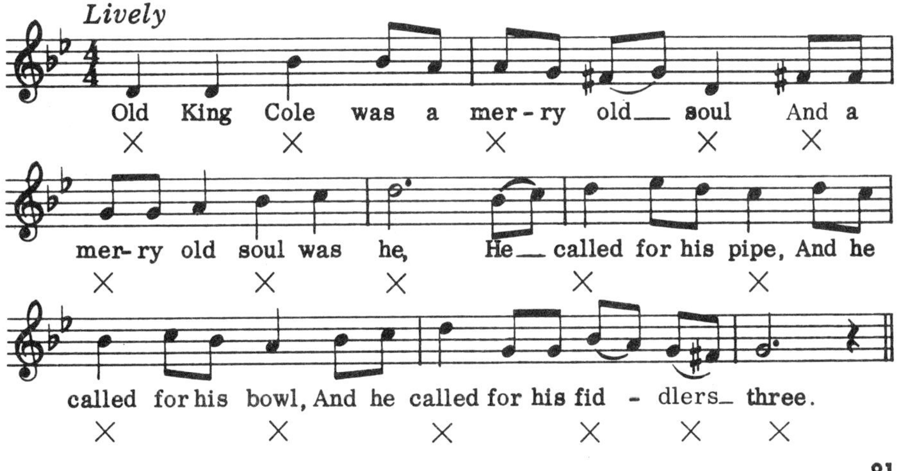

1. Change each of the following major triads to minor.

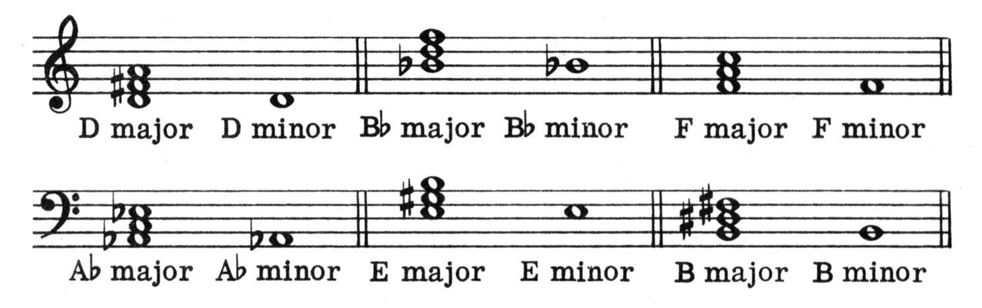

2. Write the II, III, and VI chords in the following keys.

3. Mark each chord number in "Little Jack Horner."

LITTLE JACK HORNER

Nursery Song

Moderately

Lit - tle Jack Horn - er sat in a corn - er,
I

Eat- ing his Christ-mas pie;___ He put in his thumb, and

pulled out a plum, And said, "What a good boy am I!"___
D7 G

4. Fill in the sharps or flats for the signatures of the following minor keys.

5. Name the relative minor key for each of the following major keys.

6. Harmonize on the piano the following melodies in minor keys.

CHARLIE IS MY DARLIN'

Scottish Folk Song

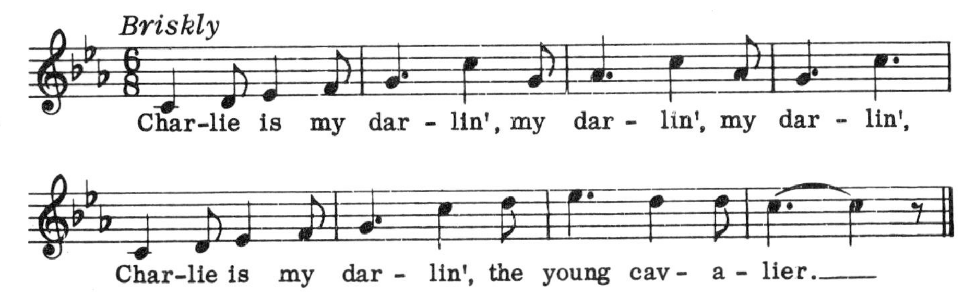

SOMETIMES I FEEL LIKE A MOTHERLESS CHILD

American Spiritual

7. Write, then play the I—IV—V_7—I chord progression in the following minor keys.

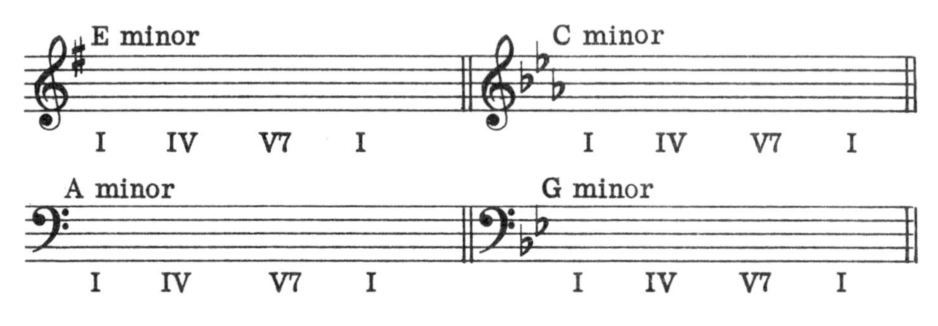

8. Improvise a period in minor, using the I, IV, and V_7 chords. You may sing your melody as you play the chords on the Autoharp, or play both melody and harmony on the piano.

9. List any additional songs you know that are in minor keys.

5

Part Singing

Part singing is one of the most spontaneous and enjoyable ways to make music in groups. Many people who have harmonized songs by the campfire or at a party may have wished for greater skill in their harmonizing. The first step in learning to harmonize with others is to sing a repeated tone against the melody. For instance, let one part of a group sing "Frère Jacques" while the other part repeats "ding dong, ding dong" on F, the key note.

FRÈRE JACQUES

French Folk Song

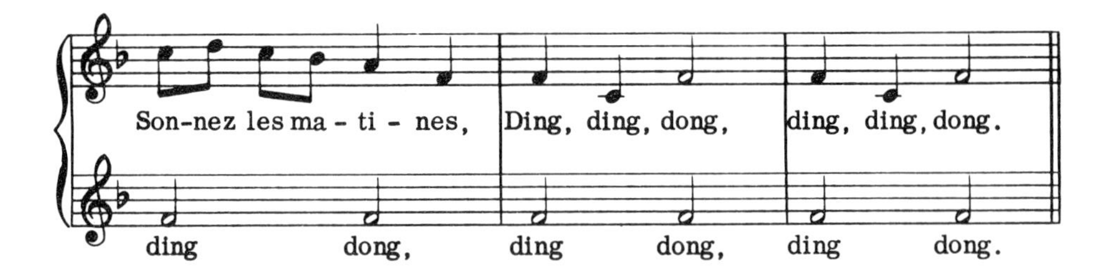

Adding Tones

Sing the song again. This time have the second group sing "ding dong" on the root and the 5th of the I chord like this:

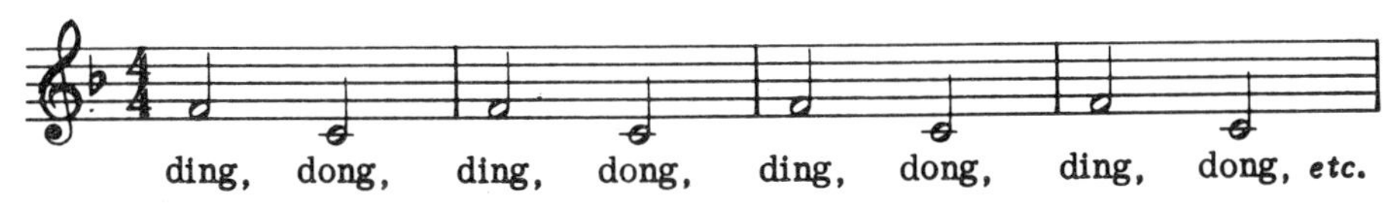

Harmonizing is essentially a process of hearing and producing the appropriate chord tones to match a melody. Singing or playing the roots of the chords against the melody, as in "Mary Had a Little Lamb," is good practice for successful part singing.

Harmonizing with 3rds and 6ths

Melodies are often harmonized by using parallel 3rds and 6ths.

A good example of this is found in "The Battle Hymn of the Republic."

Practice the ascending and descending pattern in several keys until you are proficient in singing 3rds and 6ths.

In part singing one should of course try to recognize the melodic intervals and the chord background. But he should also try to hear the tones of the lower part as another melody. In the chorus of "Liza Jane," for instance, try to hear the alto part as a lower melodic line, not as isolated chord tones of the I, IV, and V chords.

Three-Part Singing

Another way to practice part singing is to sing the I, IV, and V (or V_7) chords in three-part harmony. Divide the class into three sections, one group taking the top tone, the next group the middle tone, and the third group the lowest tone. Hum or sing the following progressions in several different keys. Use the syllable "loo."

Notice that the bottom tone remains the same, while the upper two tones move up.

Here the top tone remains the same as the two lower tones move in contrary motion.

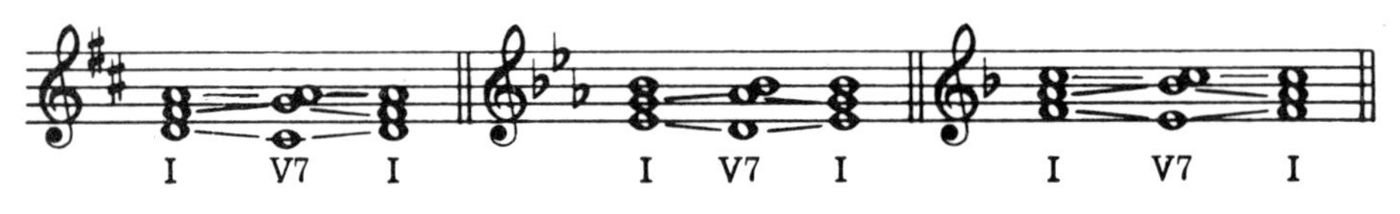

Now apply this chord background to "Silent Night." While one group sings the melody, the other group can hum the tones of the chords as indicated.

SILENT NIGHT

Joseph Mohr

Franz Gruber

Descants

To sing in true harmony with other parts, one must cultivate the ability to *listen* to his part in relation to the others. Learning to listen while you sing takes time, practice, and patience. You have already taken the initial steps by learning to add one tone against a melody and by singing in two- or three-part harmony. Now, try adding a new melody, or *descant*, above a known melody. A descant may be very simple or it may be quite elaborate, but it is fun to sing and can enhance the beauty of many songs.

Here is a simple descant to sing with the refrain of "America, the Beautiful." You may want to elaborate upon it by adding other tones, changing the rhythm, etc.

AMERICA, THE BEAUTIFUL

Katharine Lee Bates

Samuel A. Ward
Descant by Howard Murphy

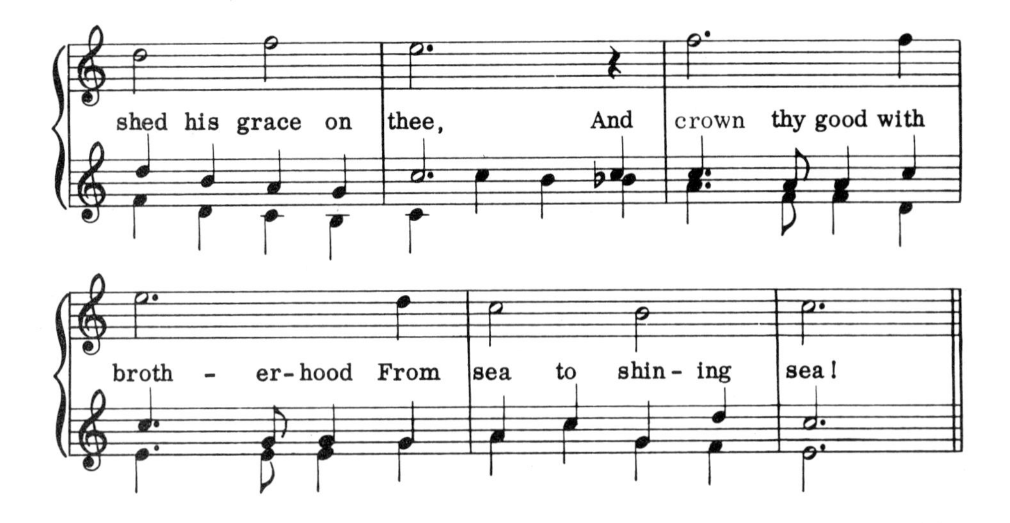

Rounds and Canons

A usual type of song for group singing is the round or canon. Familiar though it may be, the round's apparent simplicity is deceiving. Too often an inexperienced person will sing a round with a constant effort to shut out the sound of other voices so that he can stay with his own part. Very little musical value or understanding of harmony can be derived from such an experience. Well-chosen rounds can be valuable in teaching a person to *listen* while he blends his own voice with others.

A round that emphasizes chord tones, such as the following, is particularly good to initiate round singing. Each part is in harmony with the other. Divide the class into four groups, so that a new group begins singing every two measures until all four parts have entered.

WHY SHOULDN'T MY GOOSE

English Round

"Row, Row, Row Your Boat" is another good example:

ROW, ROW, ROW YOUR BOAT

Traditional

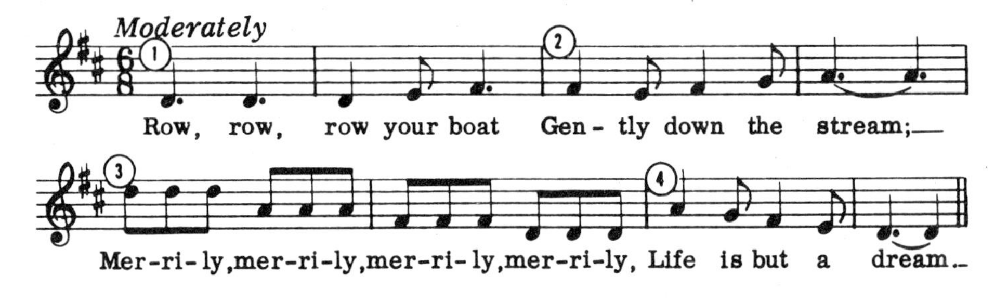

In "Sweetly Sings the Donkey" a simple harmony is created by the parallel melodic movement between the parts of the round.

SWEETLY SINGS THE DONKEY

Traditional

Lively

1 Sweet - ly sings the don - key at the break of day.

2 If you do not feed him, this is what he'll say,

3 "Hee - haw! Hee - haw! Hee - haw! Hee-haw! Hee - haw!"

The best advice for successful part singing is to be aware of the chord structure and the melodic movement, and to listen to one's part *in relation to the others.*

1. Play the melody on the bells or piano as you sing the root of the chord that harmonizes.

2. Write the tones of the I—IV—I chords in these keys. Write them both ways, first with the key signatures, and then with accidentals to make the correct chords. With other members of the class, sing the chord in three-part harmony.

3. Now follow the same procedure, using the I—V_7—I chords.

4. Sing the first two phrases of "Home, Sweet Home" in two-part harmony.

5. Mark the intervals (3rds, 4ths, etc.) between the lower and upper notes in the refrain of "Stodola-Pumpa," and sing them.

6. Fill in the missing notes in the alto part of "Santa Lucia," then sing it.

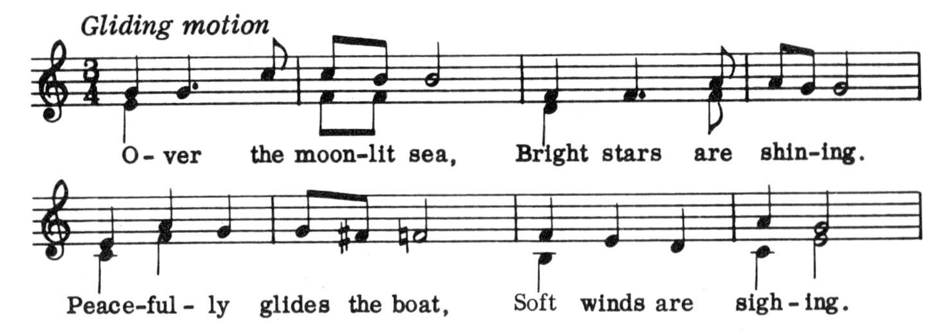

6

Altered Chords

In considering the material covered so far, you can see that knowledge of the I, IV, and V_7 chords can serve you well in your attempts to harmonize songs. It would be wrong, however, to assume that every song can be harmonized using only the I, IV, and V_7 chords. For example, "All Through the Night" contains an *altered* chord in the second measure (the tone C has been raised one half step by a sharp).

Actually, this chord becomes a dominant seventh outside the key of the song (sometimes indicated as X_7). It is therefore a "foreign" chord to this key, but one that greatly enriches the harmony.[1]

[1] The use of tones outside the diatonic scale is known as *chromaticism*. The original concept comes from the Greek word *chroma* meaning color. Therefore, chromatic tones or chords are used as musical embellishments to add color.

It is also important to realize that songs can often be harmonized in more than one style. While the chorus to "Jingle Bells" sounds all right with only the I, IV, and V_7 chords, it is much more interesting to substitute an A major chord for the V_7 in measure seven. Try it both ways.

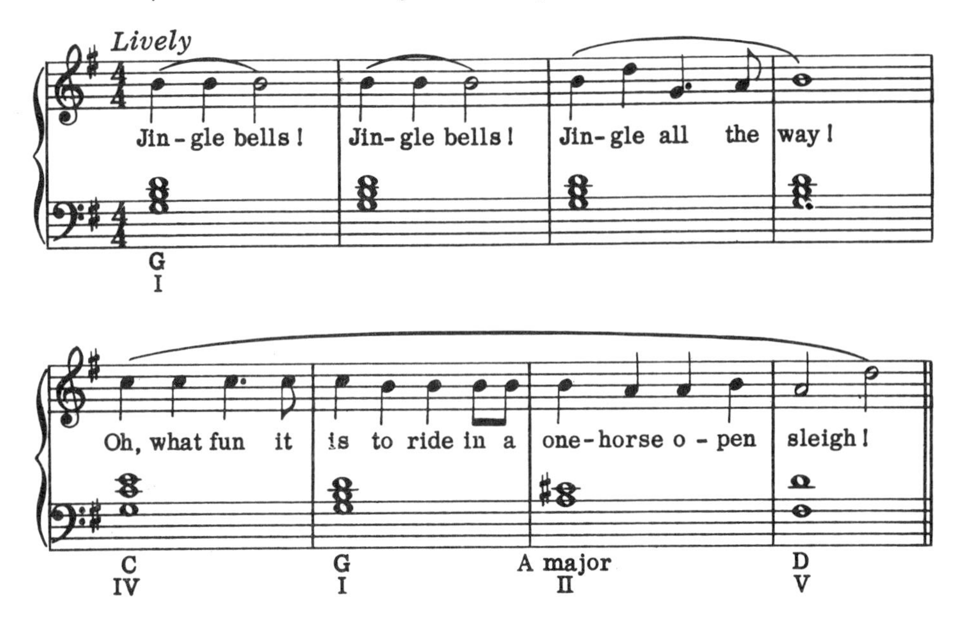

"Home on the Range" is another of the many songs that can be harmonized in more than one way.

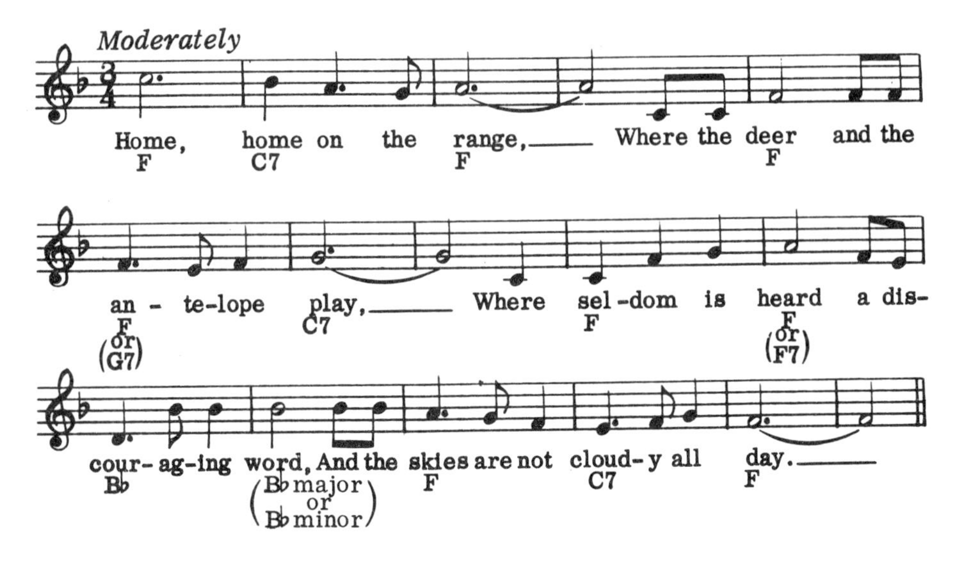

The second version borrows the G_7, F_7, and B♭-minor chords from other keys since these chords do not occur in the key of F major. Frequently, the borrowed chord is a major triad or seventh chord built on II of the scale.

Major and Minor Sonorities

Some of our most beautiful songs are those that combine major and minor sonorities in unusual ways. "Greensleeves" is a song of this type. Rather than the conventional I, IV, and V harmonization, the first part uses the E minor, D major, B minor and B major chords. The sound of the G major chord in the opening of the second part (relative major of E minor) provides exquisite tonal contrast between these two sections.

GREENSLEEVES

Traditional English

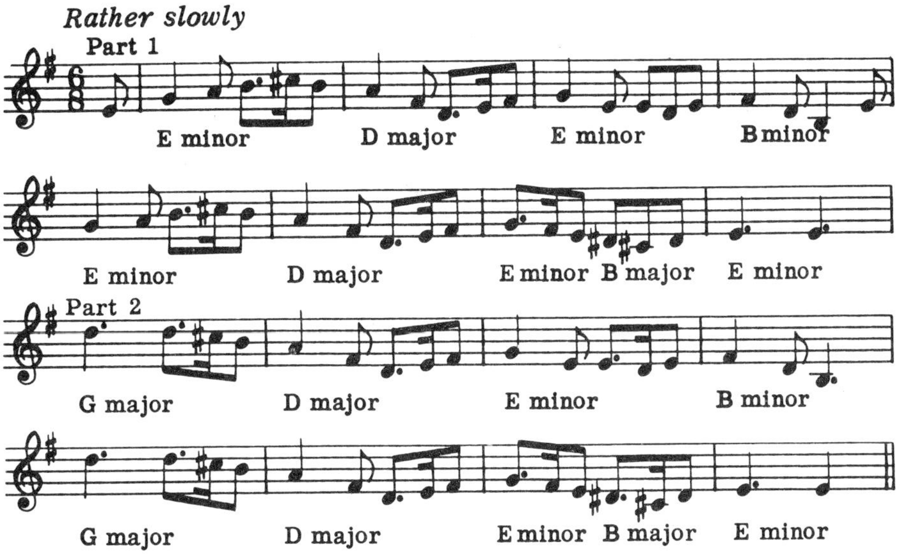

Rather slowly

Part 1

E minor D major E minor B minor

E minor D major E minor B major E minor

Part 2

G major D major E minor B minor

G major D major E minor B major E minor

Pentatonic Melodies

The *pentatonic* (five-tone) scale appears in music from many parts of the world. One easy way to identify this scale is to remember that the intervals within it are the same as those between the black keys on the piano. Sing "Auld Lang Syne" as you play the melody on the black keys of the piano.

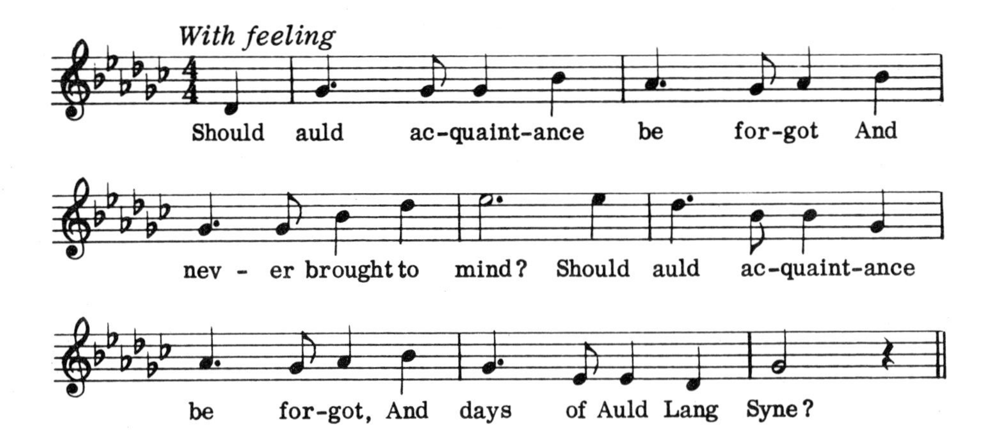

Next, add a "bagpipe" accompaniment, using these tones at the beginning of each measure:

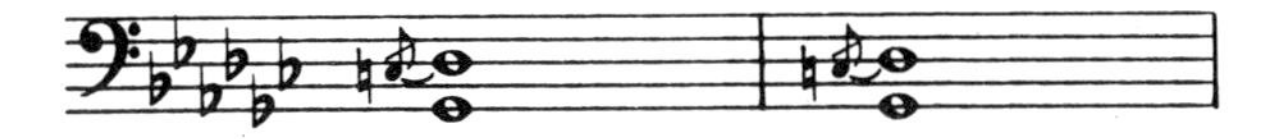

Other pentatonic melodies are found in Oriental music and in songs of the American Indians.

It is interesting to improvise melodies of this kind by using only the black keys of the piano.

FOR FURTHER STUDY

1. Circle all chromatic alterations in "Blow the Man Down."

BLOW THE MAN DOWN

Sea Chantey

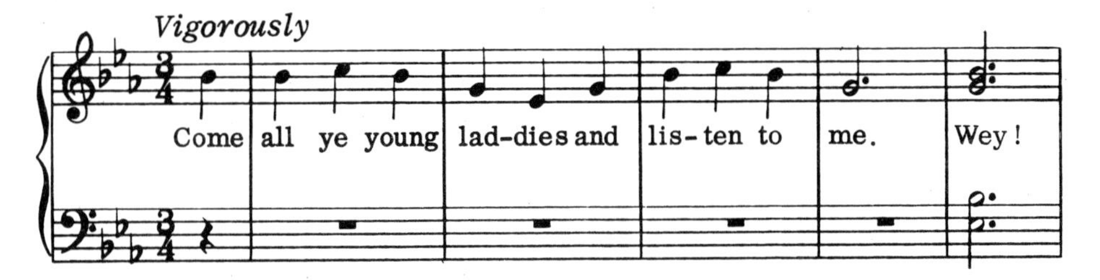

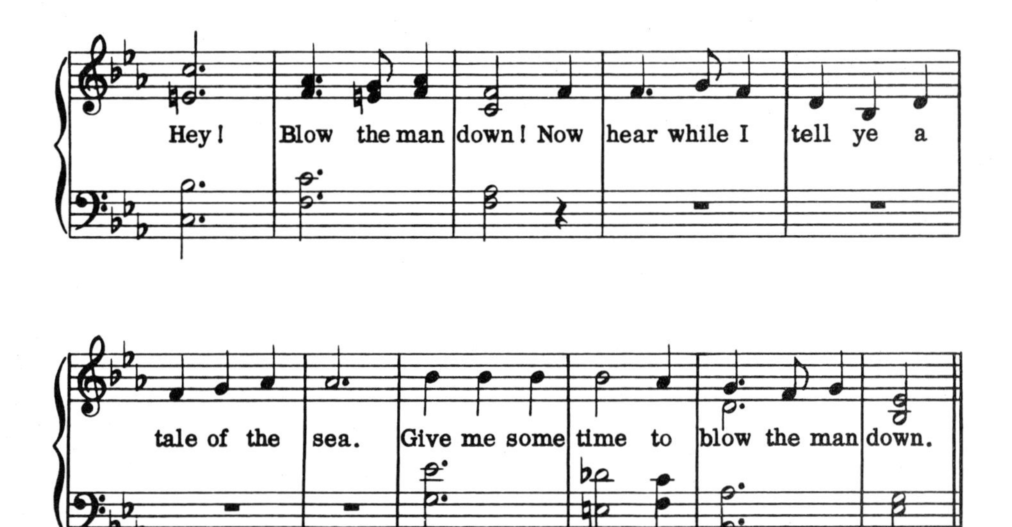

2. Harmonize "I've Been Workin' on the Railroad" by writing the letter name of the chord under each measure. You may substitute an A major, A_7, B major, or B_7 chord in the places marked by an ×.

I'VE BEEN WORKIN' ON THE RAILROAD

American Song

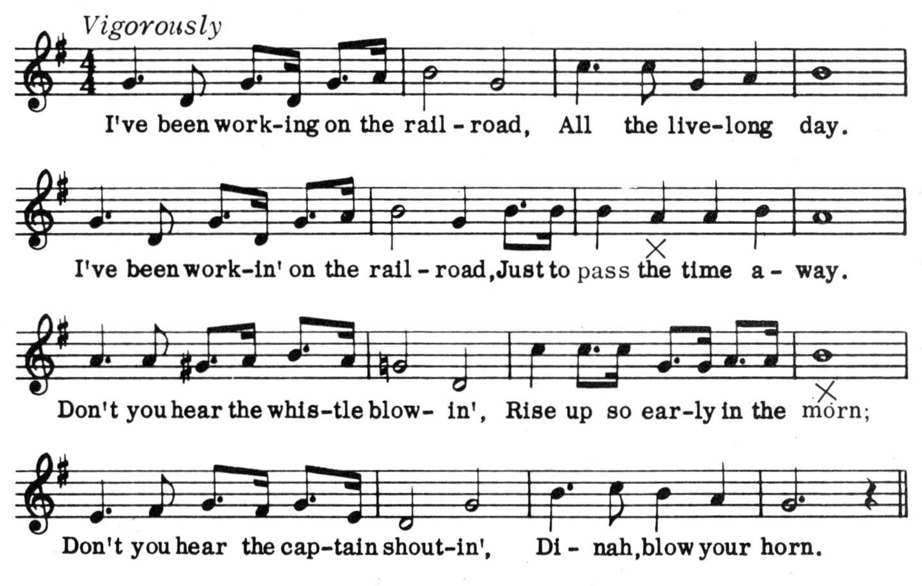

3. Harmonize "The Campbells Are Coming" with a "bagpipe" accompaniment.

Example:

THE CAMPBELLS ARE COMING

Robert Burns

Scottish Folk Song

4. On melody bells or the piano, make up melodies based on the pentatonic scale.

5. Improvise simple two-tone accompaniments for the melodies you have just created.

CONCLUDING NOTE

In this book we have analyzed some of the fundamentals of the music that we hear and sing. Although we have necessarily confined our attention to relatively few musical ideas, each example in the book is representative of many other songs and pieces of music.

The more frequently you make use of your musical knowledge, the greater your understanding and skill will become. You have learned, among other things, to read musical symbols, to make use of simple chords, and to recognize musical forms; and you have acquired a musical vocabulary.

The possibilities for increasing musical understanding are unlimited for a person who knows the structure of music. The great musicians of the past and present used just such knowledge as the basis for creating the music that we listen to. It is hoped, therefore, that this material may serve you not only as a source for increasing your professional competence, but also as an incentive toward continued musical endeavor and greater personal pleasure.

APPENDIX A
KEY SIGNATURES AND SCALES

KEY SIGNATURE	NAME OF KEY		NUMBER OF		NAME OF KEY		KEY SIGNATURE
	MAJOR	MINOR	SHARPS	FLATS	MAJOR	MINOR	
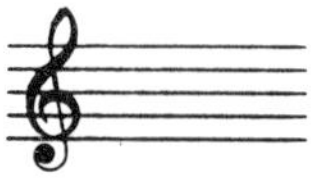	C	a	0				
	G	e	1				
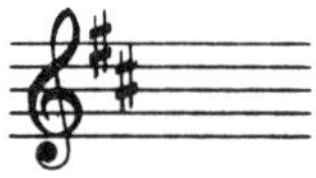	D	b	2				
	A	f♯	3				
	E	c♯	4				
	B	g♯	5	7	C♭	a♭	
	F♯	d♯	6	6	G♭	e♭	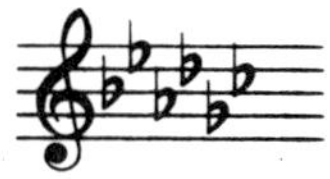
	C♯	a♯	7	5	D♭	b♭	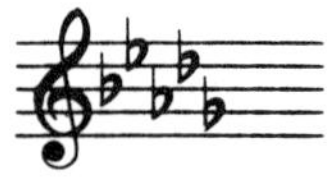
				4	A♭	f	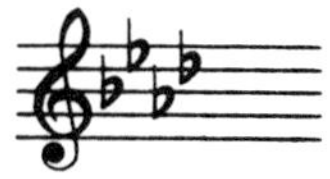
				3	E♭	c	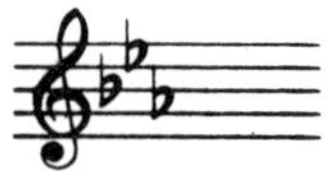
				2	B♭	g	
				1	F	d	
				0	C	a	

MAJOR AND MINOR SCALES
(SHARP KEYS)

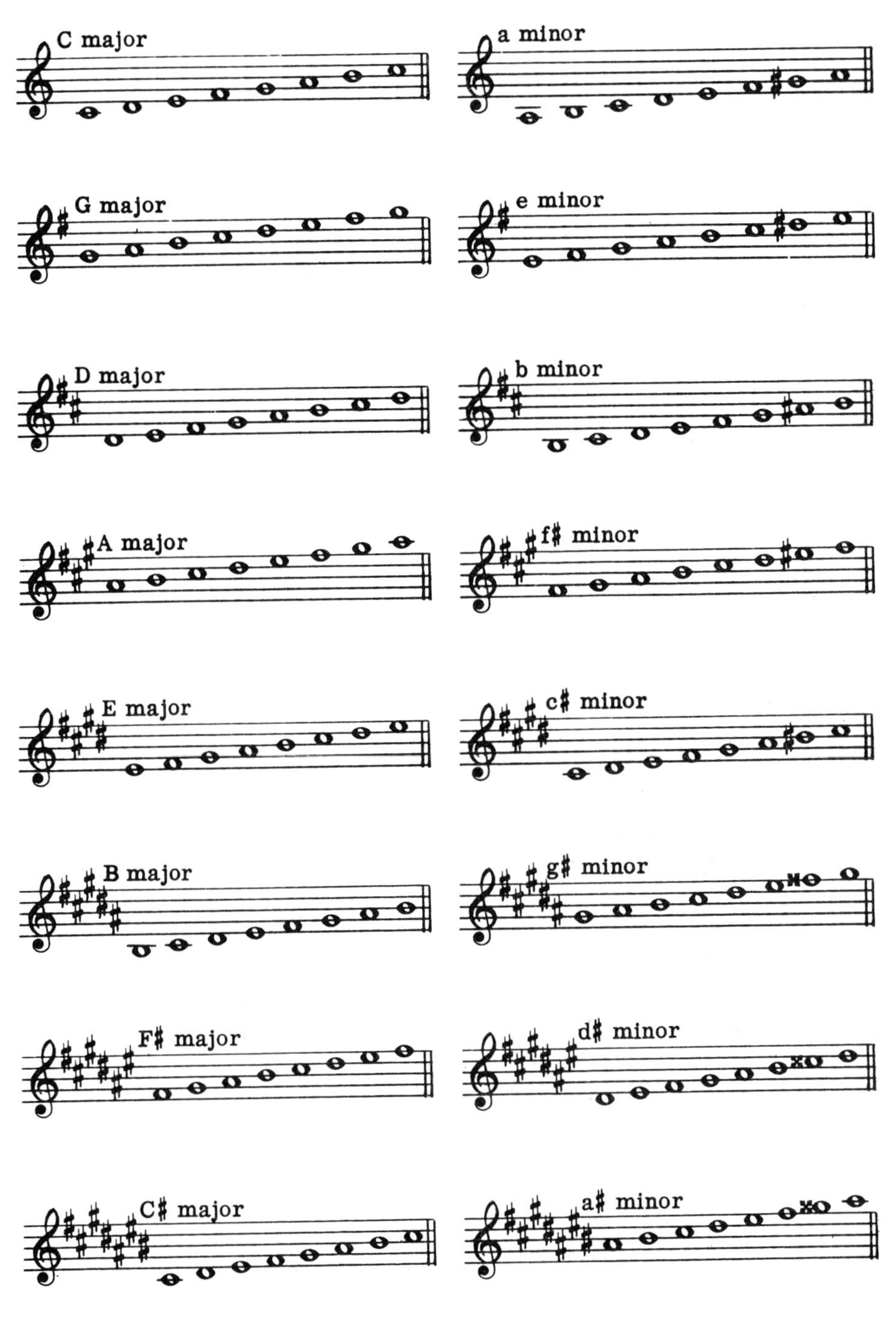

MAJOR AND MINOR SCALES
(FLAT KEYS)

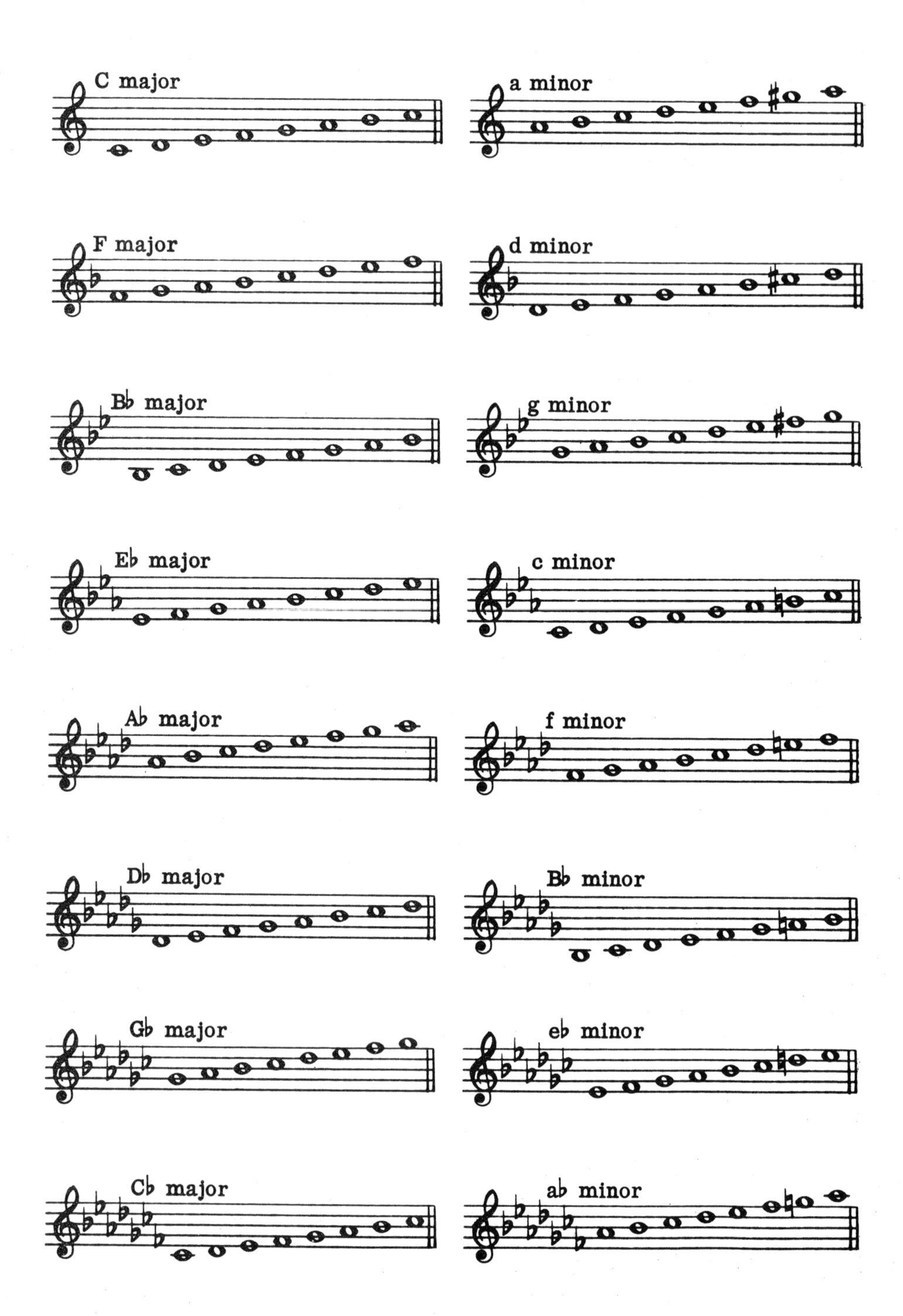

APPENDIX B
DIGEST OF FORM

CADENCES

TYPE	SYMBOL	CHORDS
Complete (ending with the root of the chord—"do"—on top)		
Perfect Authentic Cadence	‾‾‾‾‾‾‾|	V or V_7 to I
Perfect Plagal Cadence	_______|	IV to I
Incomplete (ending with the 3rd or 5th of the chord on top)		
Semicadence	‾‾‾‾‾‾‾V	ends on V or V_7
Imperfect Authentic Cadence	‾‾‾‾‾‾‾\	V or V_7 to I
Imperfect Plagal Cadence	_______\	I to IV
Evaded Cadence	_______/	V to VI

PRIMARY UNITS OF FORM

TERM AND DEFINITION

CADENCES USED

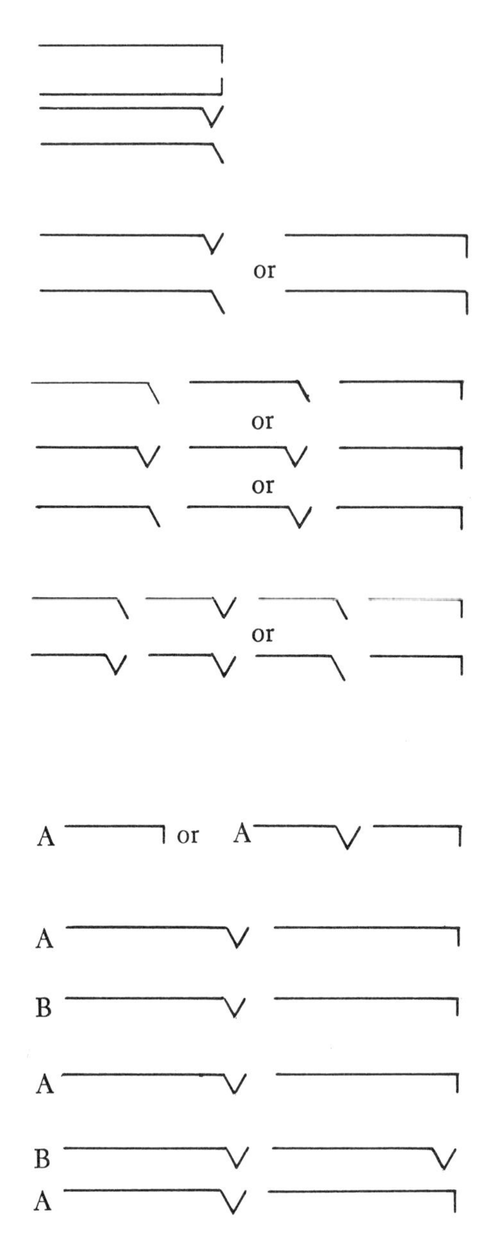

Phrase—A short musical thought

Period—Two phrases, the first giving a feeling of incompletion and the second a feeling of completion

Phrase group—Three phrases, each slightly different, ending with a perfect authentic cadence

Double period—Four phrases with a semicadence in the middle and a perfect authentic cadence at the end

SONG FORMS

One-part form—Phrase, period, double period, or phrase group

Two-part form—Part I (A) phrase or period

Part II (B) phrase or period

Three-part form—Part I (A) phrase or period

Part II (B) phrase or period

Part III (A) same phrase or period as Part I (may be modified)

APPENDIX C
SONGS

WELL-KNOWN SONGS HARMONIZED WITH THE I AND V_7 CHORDS

AIN'T GONNA RAIN
AS I WENT WALKING DOWN THE STREET
BIG CORRAL, THE
BLOW THE MAN DOWN
BRIDGE OF AVIGNON
CLEMENTINE
COBBLER, THE
COCKLES AND MUSSELS
COFFEE GROWS ON WHITE OAK TREES
COME, THOU ALMIGHTY KING
DOWN IN THE VALLEY
EENCY, WEENCY SPIDER
GEORGY PORGY
GO IN AND OUT THE WINDOW
GOING TO BOSTON?
GOIN' TO LEAVE OLD TEXAS
GO TELL AUNT RHODIE
HAIL! HAIL! THE GANG'S ALL HERE
HOT CROSS BUNS
I SEE YOU
LAZY MARY, WILL YOU GET UP?
LIGHTLY ROW
LONDON BRIDGE
LONG, LONG AGO
MARY HAD A LITTLE LAMB
MORE WE GET TOGETHER, THE
OATS, PEAS, BEANS
OLD ROGER IS DEAD
PAPER OF PINS
PAW PAW PATCH
POLLY WOLLY DOODLE
PUT YOUR LITTLE FOOT
RAIN, RAIN, GO AWAY
ROCKA-MY SOUL
SHOO FLY, DON'T BOTHER ME
SKIP TO MY LOU
SLEEPING PRINCESS
SUSIE, LITTLE SUSIE
SWEETLY SINGS THE DONKEY
TEN LITTLE INDIANS
THREE BLIND MICE
WHISTLE, DAUGHTER, WHISTLE

WELL-KNOWN SONGS HARMONIZED WITH THE I, IV, AND V_7 CHORDS

ANIMAL FAIR
AULD LANG SYNE
AUNT DINAH'S QUILTING PARTY
AWAY IN THE MANGER
BARNYARD, THE
BETSY FROM PIKE
CAMPTOWN RACES
DINAH, WON'T YOU BLOW
DRINK TO ME ONLY WITH THINE EYES
FAITH OF OUR FATHERS
FLY AND THE BUMBLE BEE, THE
FOR HE'S A JOLLY GOOD FELLOW
GLENDY BURKE
GOOD NIGHT, LADIES
HICKORY DICKORY DOCK
HOME ON THE RANGE
I SAW THREE SHIPS
JIM ALONG JOSIE
JIMMY CRACK CORN
JINGLE BELLS
LITTLE BOY BLUE
LITTLE BROWN CHURCH
LITTLE BROWN JUG
LIZA JANE
LOCH LOMOND
NEW RIVER TRAIN
O CHRISTMAS TREE
OH SUSANNA
OLD DAN TUCKER
OLD FOLKS AT HOME
OLD MACDONALD
OLD MOLLY HARE
ONE MORE RIVER
O, NO, JOHN
OVER THE HILLS AND FAR AWAY
O WORSHIP THE KING
POLLY PUT THE KETTLE ON
RED RIVER VALLEY
SHE'LL BE COMIN' 'ROUND THE MOUNTAIN
SHOEMAKER'S DANCE
SILENT NIGHT
SOLDIER, WILL YOU MARRY ME?
SOME FOLKS DO
SWING LOW, SWEET CHARIOT
THIS OLD MAN
TURKEY IN THE STRAW
TWINKLE, TWINKLE, LITTLE STAR
WABASH CANNONBALL
YANKEE DOODLE

APPENDIX D
GLOSSARY

A tempo (*ah tem′-po*)—Resume original speed after *ritardando* or *accelerando*.

Accelerando, accel. (*aht-chel-leh-rahn′-do*)—Gradually increasing speed.

Accidental—Any sign (♯, 𝄪, ♭, 𝄫, or ♮) for raising or lowering notes, not found in the signature.

Adagio (*ah-dah′-jee-o*)—Slow; slower than *andante*, but not as slow as *largo* or *lento*.

Allegretto (*ahl-leh-gret′-to*)—Slower than *allegro*.

Allegro (*ahl-leh′-gro*)—Quick, lively, vivacious.

Andante (*ahn-dahn′-te*)—Walking tempo.

Andantino (*ahn-dahn-tee′-no*)—A little faster than *andante*.

Animato (*ah-nee-mah′-to*)—With life or spirit.

Augmented interval—Any major or perfect interval increased by one half step.

Cadence (*kay′-dens*)—A rhythmic, harmonic, and melodic point of rest.

Chorale (*ko-rahl′*)—Old form of psalm tune of the German Lutheran hymn.

Chromatic (*kro-mat′-ik*)—(1) Progressing by half steps; contrasted with diatonic. (2) Involving sharps, flats, or naturals that are foreign to the key of the composition.

Clef—A sign placed on the staff to indicate the names and positions of tones. Two clefs most widely used today are:

the *treble* (G) clef

the *bass* (F) clef

Crescendo, cresc. (*creh-shen′-do*)—Becoming louder gradually.

Da Capo, D.C. (*dah-kah′-po*)—From the beginning.

Dal Segno, D.S. (*dahl-sehn′-yo*)—Repetition from the sign 𝄋

Deceptive cadence—A cadence in which the usual chord of resolution is replaced by another, giving a feeling of incompleteness; especially the progression of the V_7 to the VI.

Decrescendo, Decresc. (*deh-creh-shen′-do*)—Becoming softer gradually.

Diatonic scale (*dy-a-ton′-ic*)—The succession of eight different tones commonly referred to as major or minor scales. Diatonic of C major:

Diminished interval—Any minor or perfect interval decreased by one half step.

Diminuendo, dim. (*dee-meh-noo′-ehn′-do*)—Gradually softer.

Dominant chord—A major triad having the fifth degree of the major scale as root.

Dynamics (*dy-nam′-iks*)—Pertaining to the various levels of intensity in sounds.

Fine (*fee′neh*)—The end.

Forte, f (*for′-tay*)—Loud.

Fortissimo, ff (*for-tee′-see-mo*)—Very loud.

Grace note—A short note written thus . Technically known as acciaccatura (to crush together).

Harmony—(1) Two or more consonant pitches sounding simultaneously. (2) The art or process of combining musical sounds according to certain conventions.

Interval—The distance between two pitches, counting the lower tone as one.

Key—The relationship of tones; that grouping of tones that is drawn to.

Largo—Slow tempo.

Leading tone—The seventh degree of a scale, one half step below the key note and leading toward it. (In minor the seventh degree must be raised by an accidental to become the leading tone thereby preserving the half step relationship to the tonic.)

Legato (*leh-gah′-to*)—Smooth or connected; the opposite of staccato.

Lento (*len-to*)—Slow, between largo and adagio.

Major scale—A succession of eight tones with the following order of whole and half steps:

Major triad (*try′-ad*)—Three tones, the second and third of which are a major 3rd and a perfect 5th above the root.

Melodic interval—The distance between any two tones of a melody.

Meter—The recurrent groupings of rhythmic pulsations or beats in groups of twos and threes.

Mezzo-forte, mf (*met-tso for′-tay*)—Moderately loud.

Mezzo-piano, mp (*met′-tso pee-ah′-no*)—Moderately soft.

Minor scale—A succession of eight tones, the third degree of which is a minor 3rd above the keynote. The two commonly used ascending minor scales are:

harmonic

melodic

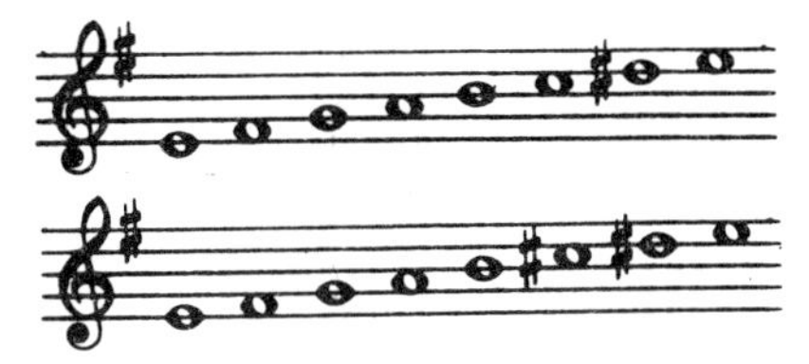

Minor triad—Three tones, the second and third of which are a minor 3rd and a perfect 5th above the root.

Modulation—Change of key or tonality.

Molto (*mol'-to*)—Much, very much.

Octave (*ahk'-tayv*)—The interval between a given tone and its repetition eight tones above or below.

Perfect interval—An interval allowing no change without destroying the consonance, such as the unison, 4th, 5th, and octave.

Pianissimo, pp (*pee-ah-nee'-see-mo*)—Extremely soft.

Piano, p (*pee-ah'-no*)—Soft.

Poco (*po-ko*)—Little.

Presto (*pres-to*)—Quickly.

Resolution—Progression from a dissonant to a consonant sound:

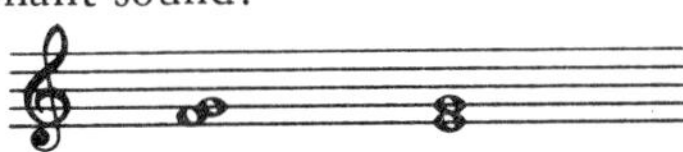

Ritardando, rit., ritard.—Getting slower.

Sequence—The repetition of a harmonic or melodic pattern on higher or lower tones.

Staccato (*stah-kah'-to*)—Separated, detached.

Suspension—A non-harmonic tone created by holding over a tone from the previous chord.

Tempo (*tem'-po*)—Rate of speed.

Theme—A melody that transmits a feeling of completeness, and serves as the basis for an extended composition.

Tonality (*tohn-al'-i-tee*)—The relationship of tones or chords to a central key tone.

Tonic (*ton'-ik*)—The principal note of the key and the first degree of the scale.

Transpose—To perform or write in another key.

Un poco (*oon-po'-ko*)—A little.

Vivace (*vee-vah'-cheh*)—Spirited, lively.

INDEX

SONGS

SUBJECTS